School-Based Instructional Rounds

IMPROVING TEACHING AND LEARNING
ACROSS CLASSROOMS

LEE TEITEL

HARVARD EDUCATION PRESS
CAMBRIDGE, MASSACHUSETTS

Library of Congress Control Number 2013939174

Paperback ISBN 978-1-61250-589-3
Library Edition ISBN 978-1-61250-590-9

Published by Harvard Education Press,
an imprint of the Harvard Education Publishing Group

Harvard Education Press
8 Story Street
Cambridge, MA 02138

Cover Design: Ciano Design

The typefaces used in this book are ITC Fenice, Minion Pro, and Myriad Pro.

To the classroom, school, and district leaders
who have embraced instructional rounds and creatively
adapted the practice into school-based settings
to help professionalize teaching and improve learning.

And, particularly, to the memory of Marilyn Oat,
the soft-spoken, thoughtful, ever-inquisitive principal
of Killingly Memorial School, who dared to ask "What if . . . ?"
and by doing so, showed how school-based
instructional rounds could dramatically improve
teaching and learning in her school.

CONTENTS

Introduction

For the last decade, an increasing number of educators have been using instructional rounds (IR) to support their efforts in school and district improvement. An idea adapted from the medical rounds that doctors use, instructional rounds helps educators look closely at the learning and teaching that is taking place in their classrooms so they can work together systematically to improve it. Rounds is typically done in networks. For example, in a cross-school network, principals and teachers from eight schools in a district might visit each school in turn over the year. Or in a cross-district network, a dozen superintendents might rotate for a monthly visit into a school in a district of one of its members. Prior to the visit, the host school and district would identify an area on which they wanted the visitors to focus—a *problem of practice*. During the visit, after the visitors have been briefed about the school context and problem of practice, they divide into groups of four or five to observe for approximately twenty minutes each in four classrooms, jotting down specific and nonjudgmental notes about what teachers and students are saying and doing. The visitors then analyze the data, looking for patterns, making predictions, and ultimately making suggestions for improvement. Members of the host school and district discuss these collegial suggestions and decide which will contribute the most to their instructional and systemic improvement. Visits are not just one-day events, but are part of the continuous improvement at the host school and district as well as the continuous learning of the network members. When rounds is working well, it enables teachers and administrators to see strong connections between their strategy and the learning that takes place in classrooms. After the publication in 2009 of *Instructional Rounds in Education: A Network Approach to Improving Teaching and Learning*, the rounds practice has grown considerably and now includes networks throughout the United States and in Canada, Australia, and Sweden.[1]

An unexpected outcome of the success of *Instructional Rounds in Education* has been the widespread interest in and use of school-based instructional rounds—a structure and approach that is barely mentioned in that book. Most of the models it describes are role-alike superintendent and principal networks, or mixed-role networks where teachers, union leaders, and administrators visit a series of schools together. A typical school in one of these networks might get visited once a year; the improvement focus for many of these networks is as much on the district, system, or the broader network as it is on any individual school.

For a significant number of schools (as well as some districts) the models for cross-site networks articulated in the 2009 book did not provide a sufficiently close and continuing focus on schools and classrooms. Educators began to experiment with and adapt the principles and practices of instructional rounds to conduct rounds repeatedly in a single-school context. Some saw developing school-based rounds as a natural progression from a rounds practice that engaged those who were relatively far from classrooms (as in a superintendent network) to one involving those closest to them (like teachers). Other districts used their district-based network as a training ground to develop norms and build the capacity of teachers and school leaders to conduct rounds, and then "graduated" them after two years to launch in-school rounds, convinced that that was where the real improvement would take place. For stand-alone schools—charters, independent schools, or schools in districts with no interest or support for rounds—rounds started as, and remained, a school-level practice.

Regardless of how they got to it, those engaged in school-based rounds, working on their own and mostly in isolation, have been developing significant variations on the rounds practice. Some have set up structures that dramatically increase the frequency of rounds visits (like the charter school that conducts rounds weekly, in contrast to the more typical monthly or bimonthly visits in cross-school settings). Others have replaced the portions of the next-level-of-work process (where visiting teams make suggestions for systemic improvement) with an internal commitment process (where school-based teacher teams decide how they want to modify their work to help address their problem of practice). In some large districts, school-based rounds visits are led by district coaches in ways that deliberately concentrate on areas of improvement that have been flagged by the district-based rounds visits. In many settings, rounds cycles are tightly tied to existing school improvement structures, where, for example, the internal teacher teams commonly involved in school-based rounds debrief their observations and analyses in professional learning communities or other meeting structures that already exist in their schools. Some districts that have encouraged, supported, or even required school-based rounds models have tried to align them with or nest them within their district-wide or cross-school rounds practices.

These emerging school-based rounds practices have a number of potential benefits. They engage teachers as major players in rounds work and related improvement efforts—something that has been difficult for some cross-district superintendent networks, or even cross-school district networks, to do successfully. The visit teams for the superintendent and principal networks and many of the district networks are composed mostly, if not completely, of administrators; so in visits in these networks, classroom teachers are much more likely to be observed than to be engaged in observing and analyzing instruction. Furthermore, because their focus is on large system improvement, cross-district or cross-school rounds practices typically focus on longer-cycle learning about larger-scale improvement, in contrast to school-based rounds practices, which tend to focus on local improvement issues. By conducting more frequent, smaller, shorter-term improvement cycles through school-based rounds, instructional improvements can be implemented and fine-tuned more regularly, with potentially speedier impacts and a greater sense of teacher and school-based efficacy. By having teachers make commitments to their peers for improvement (as opposed to or in addition to having a team of visitors make next-level-of-work suggestions) teachers and other school-based educators can develop stronger teams that tap into the power of lateral accountability.

On the other hand, we know from David Tyack and Larry Cuban, among others, that most variations on innovations tend to default back to existing norms, practices, and culture.[2] So there are potential pitfalls in the emerging school-based rounds practices. Maybe school-based rounds makes it more likely that teachers will be satisfied with the opportunity to observe each other's practice to share ideas and, in the absence of external visitors, will be less likely to work together to achieve fundamental improvement. Perhaps teachers who know each other well and have congenial relations will be more likely to stay in the "land of nice" with one another and not develop the nonjudgmental descriptive data and analysis that are the key foundations of rounds. Individual schools working in isolation may think of rounds as an observational approach, not an improvement strategy rooted in a school and district theory of action. Since a key part of the theory of action for network-based rounds is closely connected to improvement strategies at a district level, quite possibly school-based rounds will be unable to lead to any significant improvements and will just give the illusion to educators that they are conducting a practice of improvement.

OVERVIEW OF THE BOOK

This book examines and shares the hitherto isolated practices and models of school-based rounds and addresses what can be learned from them. The first section describes several representative models that have emerged, details the variations on the rounds protocols that have been implemented and why, and examines how educators in these settings are measuring impact. The second part of the book considers the possibilities presented by the school-based approach in moving the rounds practice closer to teachers and classrooms, potentially creating powerful local improvement loops and lateral accountability, and more clearly connecting rounds to other school improvement efforts. At the same time, part 2 explores concerns about the disconnection between school-based rounds and district strategy or about the possibility that the practice undermines the systemic improvement focus of network-based rounds or contributes to a bastardization of rounds that defaults to ineffective traditional norms and practices. The book concludes by identifying approaches that could be used to maximize the potential benefits of both school-based rounds and the broader instructional rounds practices.

The central argument of this book is that rounds is not a program with a rigid set of protocols, but a practice with core guiding principles and key processes that are connected to organizational strategy and theories of learning for individuals, teams, and organizations. To grow and develop a practice like this through any sort of organic evolution—to truly learn from practice—requires three things: variation, selection, and replication. The emerging school-based rounds practice provides ample examples of variation, but the *selection*—whether and how those variations improve the rounds practice—has to be determined by their impact. Educators may experiment with rounds processes and develop alternative approaches, but they always need to be checking to see if their innovations actually contribute to instructional and organizational improvement. The variations on rounds offered in this book present a chance to learn from and about school-based rounds practices and to organize and share them in ways that make it possible for educators to *replicate* them by using them to improve school-based rounds, broader network instructional rounds, and the possible connections between them.

To better understand and learn from this emerging variation, I have identified five representative school-based rounds situations. Models include rural, urban, charter, district, and independent schools, four in the United States, one in Australia. These five settings are not presented as exemplars of "perfect" school-based rounds practice. They are places that have made thoughtful and strategic investments in school-based rounds and have shown strong commitment to continued learning both about the practice and about how it contributes to instructional and organizational improvement. Each has been engaged in school-based rounds for at least three years. These schools and districts have been deliberately selected for their differences in size, organizational structure, grade level, and the students they serve. Readers are encouraged to look at the practices that have evolved in these settings and find useful learning to apply to their own.

The book is offered in the hope that it will be useful to several audiences:

- Those who are already doing, or planning to conduct school-based rounds will benefit from a book that helps with the "how-to" by sharing practices from a number of school-based settings while providing structures and framing that discourage adopting school-based rounds as an *activity*, instead of as a *practice* that keeps a focus on school (and, where appropriate) district instructional and organizational improvement.
- A wider group of educators engaged in the broader network-based rounds practice will benefit from learning ways of connecting to and engaging teachers in systematic improvement, increasing lateral accountability, exploring new roles for teachers and administrators in the practice, and making stronger connections between rounds and other school improvement work.
- Those interested in blending school-based rounds with cross-school district rounds will learn about how nested rounds can maximize the advantages of insider and outsider roles in a visit, help calibrate the practice, and help both the host school and the larger district improve.
- For those educators who are new to this work and are exploring the potential of rounds to support instructional improvement, the book will provide a variety of models and examples, as well as some criteria to assess the impacts of rounds on improvement.

ORGANIZATION OF THIS BOOK

The first part of chapter 1 provides a brief summary of the principles and practices associated with broader network rounds. This part of the chapter serves as a refresher for those who have read *Instructional Rounds in Education* and a basic primer for those who have not. The rest of the chapter provides important background about the larger purposes and practices of cross-site or network rounds in order to help frame and to understand the potential benefits and losses that the innovation of school-based rounds offers. The second part summarizes the underlying theory of action—how conducting rounds can lead to system and instructional improvement—while the third highlights the countercultural aspects of rounds and how rounds interacts with and potentially impacts the default culture that exists in most of our schools and school systems.

The next five chapters comprise part 1. Each provides a case study, including the background and context for development of school-based rounds in the setting, describing what the practice of rounds looks like—before, during, and after a rounds visit—and the relevant connections to improvement in the school and/or district. The case studies are drawn from observation, interviews, and/or written correspondence with the identified participants conducted by the author between July 2012 and February 2013.

Chapter 2 presents the case of a school in Killingly, Connecticut, a small district serving a mostly rural, poor student population. The principal of Killingly Memorial School, intrigued by the rounds process following a visit from the statewide superintendent's network, decided to modify the process to use it with the teachers in her school. She developed a variation in which half the third-grade teachers, for instance, visit the other half one week, trade places the following week, and then use grade-level team meetings to digest findings from rounds visits and make commitments to one another about the improvements that they as a team wish to implement. The cycle is repeated every seven weeks and has already led to quantifiable gains in the assessment metric used by the district for instructional rigor as well as subsequent gains by students on state test scores. Impressed with these results, the superintendent has directed each school in the district to develop its own version of school-based rounds and has modified the use of district or cross-school rounds to better coordinate and calibrate the school-based work.

Chapter 3 describes the rounds practice at Pegasus School of Liberal Arts and Sciences, a K–12 charter school in Dallas, Texas, where teacher leaders and school administrators conduct repeated three-week rotations on their problems of practice that make tight connections between rounds classroom observations and weekly staff development workshops.

Chapter 4 tells the story of the Akron Public Schools, an urban district of fifty schools that serves a student population of twenty-two thousand, approximately 70 percent of whom are eligible for free or reduced-price lunch. Akron has deliberately moved from district-based to school-based rounds as part of a conscious approach to encourage educators to reflect on and improve their practice. Over the last five years, more than half of the schools in the district have "graduated" from cross-school rounds to in-school rounds, setting the stage for reaching Akron's goal to "create a culture of educators examining their practice." At the same time, shifting rounds to be a school-based practice has highlighted for the district the variations in the capacity of its different schools to support rounds and the over-arching goal of improvement. This has led it to pay more attention to the ways in which it supports school improvement capacity and more tightly integrate that work with instructional rounds.

Chapter 5 presents the case of Farmington Public Schools, a small, relatively affluent school district in Connecticut that has been engaged in instructional rounds practice for over nine years and uses school-based rounds along with district-based and vertical rounds as integral parts of its school and district improvement strategy.

Chapter 6 looks at Ballarat Clarendon College, an independent K–12 school in Australia that, after participating in one of the Harvard Graduate School of Education's Instructional Rounds Institutes, embraced rounds as a way to improve instruction and reduce the variation in quality of teaching in its classrooms. After over two years of slowly and steadily scaling up the rounds practice to include almost its entire faculty, BCC took a thoughtful and deliberate pause to refine its practice and to make adaptations to better connect rounds with the evolving school improvement strategy. The BCC story is deliberately placed as the last case in part 1, since the very thoughtful reflective work done by the rounds leaders at the school makes the case an excellent transition to part 2.

Part 2, comprising chapters 7, 8, and 9, cuts across all the cases and focuses and reflects on the potential benefits of school-based rounds in contributing to improvement at the school level (and where appropriate, district level). Chapter 7 examines the implications of conducting rounds practice in the immediacy and intimacy of a school setting, where everybody knows everybody else and everyone shares the same context, structures, and culture. Chapter 8 looks at how tighter connections between rounds practice and other school-based improvement efforts, including data improvement cycles and teams and professional learning communities, can provide for clearer and more coherent structures and systems for improvement. Chapter 9 explores the changing role of teachers as they become engaged as partners in, and not just recipients of, repeated, continuous cycles of instructional improvements. The chapter reflects on how this change contributes to the development of a sense of collective efficacy and in some cases leads to new roles and relationships between and among teachers and administrators.

Each chapter also includes questions, concerns, and challenges that are raised by these same innovations, exploring the possibility that each potential benefit may also have a downside and might actually be detrimental to school and district improvement. Each ends with suggestions that might serve to minimize the concerns and maximize the potential benefits.

The conclusion of the book dives deeper into the advantages and disadvantages of school-based rounds, exploring what can be learned from sharing these practices in ways that can help those implementing school-based rounds, as well as for those interested in or engaging in the broader network practice. An appendix follows that serves as a guide to reflecting on and improving rounds practice and creating or improving the use of school-based rounds as part of a nested system.

PART I

Case Studies

CHAPTER 1

Overview of Instructional Rounds

Practice, Impact, and Philosophy

Principal Randall Lewis stood at the front of the school library.[1] Members of his district's instructional rounds network had gathered there for coffee, muffins, and conversation before the official start of the day's visit: "Welcome to Jefferson Middle School. We're excited to have you here today to help us with our problem of practice. We're also a little nervous, but that's okay. I've told the teachers that this is about my learning and the network's learning, and that we're going to get lots of good information from having so many eyes and ears in our classrooms."

Randall described the problem of practice on which he and the teachers had asked the visitors to focus: "Last spring, we rolled out a new literacy initiative that required a radical shift in teaching strategies for many of our teachers. A year later, we're trying to understand what we've learned and what we haven't, and whether it's translating into different kinds of learning for students." As participants found and greeted the other members of their observation team and gathered maps and papers for notes, there was a buzz of anticipation—much like a group of scientists about to embark on fieldwork for data collection.

Randall Lewis and his colleagues are about to spend the day doing something that many educators have never done—something that is at the heart of this book. They will be going on an instructional rounds visit—looking at classroom instruction in a focused, systematic, purposeful, and collective way. The goals of their observation are not to provide supervision or evaluation for specific teachers, but to look closely at what is happening in their schools' classrooms and to work together systematically to try to provide high-quality teaching and learning for all their children. Along with other principals, teachers, union leaders, and central office personnel, Lewis is learning about improving instructional practice by participating in instructional rounds, an idea adapted from the medical rounds model used by doctors.

In most settings, rounds is a network practice that brings together educators from across schools within a district or across districts to work together on instructional improvement. Rounds participants represent all types of educators. Historically, the networks began with of superintendents in Connecticut and Iowa, principals in Massachusetts, and mixed teams (superintendents, chief academic officers, union leaders, teachers, and principals) in Ohio and have spread to include role-alike and mixed networks throughout the United States and in Canada, Australia, and Sweden. More recently, school-based versions of the rounds practice have emerged, sometimes within larger district settings and sometimes for stand-alone schools, like charter or independent schools.

This chapter provides an overview of the instructional rounds practice in three parts. The first focuses on what rounds is, using the Jefferson Middle School example to provide the basics of what typically happens before, during, and after an instructional rounds visit. The second part summarizes the underlying theory of action—how conducting rounds can lead to system and instructional improvement. The third part highlights the countercultural aspects and potential impacts of rounds on the top-down compliance-oriented default culture that exists in most schools and school systems.

THE PRACTICE: OVERVIEW OF THE ROUNDS PROCESS

The focused and purposeful work that takes place at a visit like the one at Jefferson takes some getting used to. It helps to think about rounds as having three recurrent parts in an overall improvement cycle: the work that is done before the visit, the visit itself, and the follow-up work after the visit. It also helps to think about how the visit supports the improvement cycle for the host school as well as for the network.

Before the Visit

Before the visit, staff of the host school reflect on the improvement work that they are already trying to do, look at their student data, and identify a *stuck point*—where the adults in the building feel less effective than they wish to be in supporting student learning. This becomes the *problem of practice* on which they ask members of the network to focus during classroom observations. The problem of practice centers on instruction and is observable in classrooms. It should be something that the host school sees as high leverage and on which the team is genuinely stuck and looking for help. At the Jefferson School, Lewis and his staff had spent a year's worth of professional development trying to weave literacy strategies into their classrooms and were wondering why students didn't seem to be benefiting from them. (See exhibit 1.1 for additional examples of problems of practice.)

The more engaged the staff is in the development of the problem of practice, the greater the likelihood is that the rounds visit will contribute to school improvement. Consequently, many schools use faculty meetings, instructional leadership

---

EXHIBIT 1.1

Additional examples of problems of practice

Example 1

Seventy percent of our students in special education did not pass the state test last year. In particular, they did not do well on the open-ended questions in both math and English language arts. In many cases, they left those problems blank. We may not be providing these students with enough practice on open-ended questions. We may be providing too much assistance so that when they have to tackle these prompts on their own, they do not know where to start.

Focus questions:
• What kinds of tasks are students being asked to do?
• What are the different ways you see students begin assigned work in class?

Example 2

On the state assessment, most students are passing, but only half of the students are in the proficient category, with few in advanced. Data analysis shows that across content areas students are scoring lower on open-ended questions than short-answer or multiple-choice questions, which is consistent with what teachers notice on class work. Students struggle with independently articulating their thinking and applying their learning in new contexts.

Focus questions:
• What is the task?
• In what ways do you see of students articulating their thinking orally or in writing?

teams, and other ongoing school structures to help identify an issue that is truly owned by and of concern to the staff. If there are already strong school improvement processes in place, often the problem of practice for a visit will draw from and connect with them. In addition, before the visit many schools will provide some sort of exposure and optional training in the process for school staff. Since rounds takes a very different approach than traditional top-down administrative walkthroughs, is very helpful if, before the visit, teachers understand the nonjudgmental, collegial nature of the visit. Teachers who are involved in identifying the problem of practice, care about it, and understand the purpose and the processes of the rounds visit are much more likely to learn from the results, as opposed to feeling judged by them.

Prior to a visit, a network may explore challenges shared by its members and agree on a common focus for the year. For example, in its first year, the Ohio Leadership Collaborative, comprising mixed teacher and leadership teams from five districts, decided to focus on a broad common issue—the teaching and learning being done in each of the districts to support higher-order thinking skills. This not only shaped the visits that took place over the year, but also became the focus for reading, discussion, and other professional development that the network members undertook to support their learning. It required educators from all the districts to calibrate—to agree in a very descriptive level on what students and teachers would be doing in classrooms that exhibited different levels of higher-order thinking. Networks will also typically work both before and after visits to hone and improve the rounds and improvement practices that they use, to maximize their learning as a network, and to maximize the impact of each visit on their member schools and districts.

At the Visit

On the visit day, the problem of practice is shared with the visitors at the start of the day, along with background information and context about the school that will help the visitors make sense of their observational data and make more specific and targeted suggestions at the end of the day. Typically, Randall Lewis and a team of teachers from the school might take thirty to forty-five minutes at the beginning of the day to explain the problem of practice, where it came from, what data led to it, what the school has already done to address it, and where the school feels stuck. If time permits, they will also give some background information about the school's improvement processes—its teaming structures, how it uses data, and when and how professional development takes place. Visitors will have time for clarifying questions and to make sure they are calibrated on what kind of data to collect during their observations.

A central part of any visit is the *observation of practice*. Typically groups of four or five visitors will observe in four classrooms for about twenty minutes each. The classrooms are selected by the host site to reflect the problem of practice. Since Jefferson's literacy strategies were supposed to be embedded in all classes, the visits covered a wide range of classrooms and grades. In another setting, a focus on mathematics might bring visitors to a narrower group of classes. Observers learn to take careful descriptive notes, and to pay special attention to students and the tasks they are doing—not just what students are being *asked* to do, but what they are *actually* doing. Because in their networks, visitors will already be familiar with the instructional core—the interconnections between the work of students and teachers in the presence of content—they will not just be looking at what teachers do, but observing and talking to students and looking at the work they are doing. The visitors are guided by the host school's problem of practice. At Jefferson, the team was given a one-page summary of fourteen literacy strategies that teachers had been trained to use and were asked to look for evidence and patterns of student use of these strategies.

The next step of the rounds process is the *observation debrief*, in which participants sift through the evidence they collected together. There are three stages in the debrief process: description, analysis, and prediction. The *description* stage keeps the focus on a factual description of what visitors actually saw—not their reactions, judgments, or inferences. Typically observers, who have taken copious detailed and specific notes during their observations, sit quietly for ten to fifteen minutes to select data from their notes that they think would be particularly useful in focusing on the problem that the school has identified. They transfer the selected, focused data to sticky notes, which they share with their fellow observers. Colleagues will give feedback on these notes to ensure that they are specific and nonjudgmental before moving forward to the next step—the *analysis* stage of the debrief—where they look for patterns within and across the classrooms they saw. In this step and throughout the process, the visitors are aggregating up—focusing not so much on the practices they saw in any one class as on looking across classes to see what they notice about, for instance, the use of literary strategies (as at Jefferson).

Groups then build on these patterns to move to the *predictive* stage of the debrief, where the goal is to connect teaching and learning. Participants ask themselves,

"Given the patterns that we have just seen, if you were a student at this school and did everything you were expected to do, what would you know and be able to do?" By linking the task and teacher's instruction directly to student learning, network members tackle the central question, "What causes the learning we want to see?" What specific teaching moves, what kinds of tasks, what forms of student engagement lead to powerful learning for students? This process ultimately helps participants identify potential areas for improvement and offers clues about *how* these areas could be improved, including the specific strategies and techniques that teachers could use and what the school or district could do to support them. Taken cumulatively, these debrief practices allow participants to describe the specific behaviors and structures they see that cause, enable, or at times constrain learning.

At Jefferson, the patterns that emerged in the *analysis* section of the debrief were clear and quite consistent across the dozens of classrooms visited. Visitors saw teacher use of one or more of the literacy strategies, but they saw almost no independent student use of the strategies. This led to the *prediction* that students in these classes would be able to follow directions in using specific literacy strategies *when asked to do so by their teacher.*

The final step of the rounds process on the day of the visit is identifying the *next level of work*, when network members think together about what kinds of resources and supports teachers and administrators would need in order to move instruction to the next level. (We use that particular phrase *next level of work* because school improvement is not a linear process. There are often flat points or plateaus—or even dips—along with rises on the journey to improvement. The phrase acknowledges that the work that the school has already done to get to their current position may need to change in order to get it to reach the next level.) Here again, the more specific and precise the suggestions, the more helpful they are. At Jefferson, the visitors suggested that the school be more explicit with students about the goal of having them using these strategies in their own reading, writing, and thinking. Concrete suggestions included giving students a version of the one-page summary of literacy strategies and having them track their own use of these strategies, combining this with teaching students about metacognition and making explicit to students and teachers alike that the goal was to have students use the strategies, not just teachers. In this particular example, most of the suggestions were based at the school level, because they involve improvements and interventions that were doable with the current resources at the school. In other cases, visitors on rounds may make specific suggestions that can be addressed at the district level as well.

After the Visit

Arguably, the most important part of the improvement cycle takes place after the visit. Teachers and administrators at the host school and district need to make sense of the observations, patterns, predictions, and advice that the visitors have left them. They need to make plans to translate the learning that they have received that day into action in ways that connect with and support the ongoing improvement efforts at the school and in the district. They also need to figure out how to engage all members of the faculty in these improvement efforts—not just the handful who have been on the visit. At the same time, the network needs to consolidate and incorporate its learning from the visit into its ongoing improvement work.

After the visit at Jefferson, not only were members of the staff making plans to implement the suggestions arising from the visit, but teachers and administrators from other schools and districts in the network discussed how they could improve the specificity of their guidance to and support of students in learning in other content areas. Administrators from Jefferson's district discussed what they had learned about how they could better support literacy work in all their schools. Lewis knew that at the next network meeting, he and the teachers from the school would be expected to share briefly with the network how the findings from the visit had been shared with the faculty and what specific follow-up steps were being taken. Some networks, in recognition of the importance of follow-up and the ways hosts and visitors continue to learn from the leadership moves that follow visit, have set up mini-revisits by a subset of the network. For example, in the Connecticut Superintendents' Network, within three months of the network visit, two peer superintendents will come back to the school and the district for half a day to discuss the follow-up.

In instructional rounds work, the school visit always gets the most attention. It is a high-energy event that brings insiders and outsiders to the school together to do some observations, patternmaking, and deep collegial problem-solving. But the visit can never stand alone. It should be understood as a key and highly visible part of the improvement process for the host school and for the network (see exhibit 1.2). The rounds visit supports the learning cycle of the network and the host.

ACCELERATING INSTRUCTIONAL IMPROVEMENT

The goal in doing instructional rounds work is to help schools and districts develop effective and powerful teaching and learning at scale—not just isolated pockets

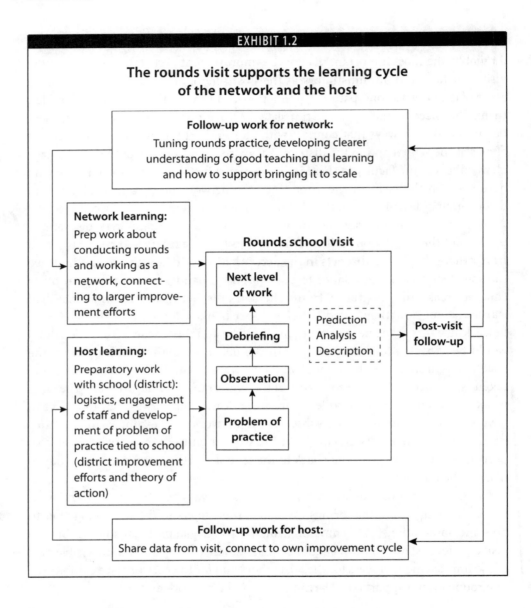

EXHIBIT 1.2

The rounds visit supports the learning cycle of the network and the host

Follow-up work for network:
Tuning rounds practice, developing clearer understanding of good teaching and learning and how to support bringing it to scale

Network learning:
Prep work about conducting rounds and working as a network, connecting to larger improvement efforts

Rounds school visit

Next level of work

Prediction
Analysis
Description

Post-visit follow-up

Debriefing

Observation

Host learning:
Preparatory work with school (district): logistics, engagement of staff and development of problem of practice tied to school (district improvement efforts and theory of action)

Problem of practice

Follow-up work for host:
Share data from visit, connect to own improvement cycle

of good teaching in the midst of mediocrity. Accordingly, at a rounds visit, the network's suggestions for the next level of work are never about "fixing" any one teacher or group of teachers. They are about developing clarity about good instructional practice and about the leadership and organizational practices needed to support this kind of instruction at scale. Suggestions in typical cross-site network rounds for the next level of work are, if anything, intended more for administrators and other leaders than for individual teachers.

How does this bring about improvement? People often ask us, "Will doing rounds lead to an increase in student learning? Will it raise test scores?" The short answer is: By itself, no. The rounds process is not a silver bullet that will single-handedly lead to better test scores or increased learning for students, but it *is* a powerful accelerant of school and district improvement efforts. Districts and schools that are improving teaching and learning at scale have developed three things:

- A clear idea about what high-quality teaching and learning should look like
- A coherent and strategic approach to systemic improvement
- A collaborative approach to adult learning that is embedded in practice and relies on engagement and inquiry rather than compliance

Although these sound relatively simple, each actually requires deep cultural change as educators need to learn new ways of working with one another.

A Clear Idea About What High-Quality Teaching and Learning Should Look Like.   Getting agreement on what high-quality teaching and learning look like is a complex, value-laden task and moves educators away from the atomized individual practice that, for many, is the cherished norm. The rounds visits focus on what goes on in classrooms and anchor improvement efforts in the instructional core—the complex relationships among teachers, students, and content. The calibration that takes place in visits forces educators to define more clearly what they mean. Unlike many educators who call for "increased rigor" or "critical thinking skills" with only a vague idea of what these terms mean, rounds network members work together to develop detailed lists of what those abstract ideas should look like in real classrooms—agreeing on what teachers and students would be saying and doing if critical thinking skills were being demonstrated, or what students would be working on if their tasks were really rigorous. And when they don't see these signs of critical thinking or rigor, they don't blame teachers, students, parents, or other external factors; instead, they look within the school and district to suggest new and powerful ways educators can work together to achieve the high student learning outcomes they desire.

A Coherent and Strategic Approach to Systemic Improvement.   Getting strategic and coherent is a major departure for many systems. It is more common for a school district (and even a school) to have a variety of loosely connected initiatives without clear feedback loops on their efficacy in impacting what happens in the classroom. The rounds process encourages educators to use *theories of action* to articulate and then test causal connections between a given improvement initiative and the impact that it has in classrooms on learning and teaching.

Rounds encourages people to state their theories of action as *if-then* propositions, in part to stress the causal nature of the statements and in part to reinforce the idea that these are testable propositions that should be subject to revision if the educators are working hard at learning their practice. For example, under the overall goal of increasing literacy in Jefferson Middle School's district, the school itself developed a theory that might be articulated as, "If we teach teachers literacy strategies to teach their students, then student skills at reading in all their classes across the curriculum will improve, contributing to their overall improved learning." (This is a school theory of action; for other examples, see exhibit 1.3.)

Through its close look at classrooms, rounds provides a key source of data and a powerful feedback loop to tell educators whether their improvement efforts are actually reaching students and, if not, how to modify the efforts to achieve better effects. In the Jefferson example, the school learned that parts of its theory of action were working—teachers had learned the literacy strategies and were teaching them to their students. There was, however, a break in the chain, since the students seemed to be using the strategies only when directed by a teacher. By making this theory explicit and visible to the observers, the rounds visit helped the school identify next steps in addressing the weak links of the causal chain

A Collaborative Approach to Adult Learning.   A collaborative approach to adult and organizational learning is one that embeds adult learning into practice and relies on engagement and inquiry rather than compliance. For many schools and school systems, this is an enormous shift in culture. It requires moving from a top-down hierarchical system in which administrators and other outside "experts" make the important instructional decisions and then check to ensure that teachers are implementing them. It suggests new roles for administrators in relationship to teachers, and to teachers in relationship to each other and to new systems of vertical and lateral accountability. It requires changes in deep-seated norms of practice, moving learning in schools and school systems from a primarily individual, isolated activity to a collective activity that can be examined, discussed, and improved.

Because of its nonjudgmental, descriptive approach, which separates the person from the practice, rounds makes it easier for professional learning to occur. Trust and a sense of collective efficacy are key elements for organizational and instructional improvement. The shared experience in rounds of developing a common language for describing and analyzing instructional practice and common norms for collective learning creates opportunities for the development of trust. Repeated

---

EXHIBIT 1.3

Two theories of action: From a district and a school within it

The first excerpt is one of four bullets from the Farmington District theory of action, circa 2009. The second is the one of five bullets in the school-based theory of action most related to that district bullet; followed by the detailed initiatives put into place to support it.

Farmington District theory of action (excerpt)

If I/we cultivate expertise in teaching and learning as the means for improving student achievement, then teaching will be strengthened and more students will learn in deeper ways that better approach the "essential understanding" of the standards.

School-based theory of action (related excerpt)

Peter J. Cummings, EdD, Principal, West Woods Upper Elementary School

If we continually develop the instructional expertise of our teachers, then teaching will be strengthened and all students will learn in deeper and more meaningful ways.

- We will embed ongoing professional development in our regular schedule (content area meetings, team meetings, faculty meetings) and specifically develop teachers' pedagogical content knowledge in reading, writing, math, science, and social studies.
  ◦ Sixth-grade content area meetings in writing and math
  ◦ Faculty meeting devoted to instructional practice
- We will work with resource teachers to develop and implement specific content models of good instruction tailored to the upper elementary level.
  ◦ Developing concepts of Teaching for Understanding through collaborative coaching and implementation of new curricula
  ◦ Creating and coordinating professional development so that there is a common focus on the "big ideas" of upper elementary instruction, while exploring how instruction should be tailored to content in each area
- We will work with team leaders to develop their group facilitation skills and implementation of a collaborative planning model.

Source: Adapted with permission from Elizabeth A. City, Richard F. Elmore, Sarah E. Fiarman, and Lee Teitel, *Instructional Rounds in Education* (Cambridge, MA: Harvard Education Press, 2009), 47–48.

practice of instructional rounds creates collective efficacy among teachers and administrators around student learning. The collaborative learning approach used in rounds networks creates norms that support adult learning and make organizational learning possible, but a great deal of change in the default culture has to take place for this to happen.

ROUNDS AS A COUNTERCULTURAL PRACTICE: BUILDING EDUCATION AS A PROFESSION

Instructional Rounds in Education is a practical, how-to book; at the same time, it is a visionary book that makes clear that we see rounds as a way to professionalize educator practice, to move from the default culture of teachers and administrators mostly operating in a bureaucratic and compliance-oriented culture to "a profession, with a shared set of practices, a body of collective knowledge, and a set of mutual commitments that define professional accountability."[2]

In the four years since the publication of the book, as we have worked in ongoing ways with multiple networks involving dozens of school systems, my colleagues and I have seen a great deal of progress. We have been privileged to work with hundreds of educators who have imaginatively, creatively, and diligently used the rounds practice to improve instruction in their own settings. And when we check in periodically to find out what is working well and what is not, we have learned a great deal that has improved the way we teach and think about instructional rounds practice. We are hopeful about and encouraged by this progress.

We've also seen the power and resiliency of the default culture, having witnessed a number of the districts that have gotten very good at "doing" rounds but are not getting the consequent improvements that could be coming from the practice. As we have worked closely with these districts to understand what is happening and what isn't, we have noticed a number of patterns that are helpful to keep in mind as part of the framing for this book on school-based rounds.

Some of these patterns can be tied to the three qualities of high-performing school districts discussed above—agreement on what high-quality teaching and learning should look like, a strategic and coherent approach to improvement, and a collaborative approach to adult and organizational learning. Others have more to do with the instructional rounds practice and how it has been implemented in these settings:

- Of these three qualities of high-performing school districts, probably the most progress has been made in developing and articulating clear ideas about what high-quality teaching and learning should look like. Whether they have adapted or adopted existing frameworks like those of Charlotte Danielson, more districts have developed these and are starting to use them.
- There's certainly been some progress in the districts with which we work in their development of a coherent and strategic approach to systemic

improvement. Some have used the theory-of-action idea to effect positive change. Some have used it side by side with *Strategy in Action* or with other coherence-making approaches like that of *Data Wise*.[3] But what many of them have found is that an improvement strategy is more than a blueprint or set of ideas that lives in the heads of system and school leaders. It has to include the organizational capacity to deliver on the promise of improvement. In the last few years, they—and we—have gotten clearer about what that improvement capacity needs to look like at the school level. Factors like instructional leadership, teaming structures, availability and use of data, collaborative engagement of teachers and administrators in the work of improvement, and a concomitant sense of efficacy and accountability are critical. When schools have well-developed capacity in these areas *and* a clear understanding of what good teaching and learning look like, it is much more likely that a strategy developed in the system can actually be enacted at the school and classroom level.

- The norms about adult and organizational learning have proven very difficult to change. Our culture is very strongly oriented around a *status* mind-set that can best be summarized as the belief that, when it comes to a knowledge, skill, or individual or organizational attribute, "you either have it or you don't." This stands in sharp contrast to a more *developmental* approach, which acknowledges the gradual and sometimes incremental learning that characterizes individual and organizational growth in other settings.[4] And, although our colleagues in schools and districts report some progress in "separating the person from the practice" and getting educators to move out of the "land of nice" to actually name and address the real challenges and stuck points they face, the analyses often don't go below the surface and the norms for follow-up still need to be strengthened. Rather, while educators seem pleased to be able to see and learn from each other's practice (and consequently enjoy and are enthusiastic about participating in rounds), the next-level-of-work suggestions are often not as deep and context specific as they could be.

- Through the continued work in these networks, we've also noticed several other patterns relating to the rounds practice itself:
  - An over-focus on the visit, and not enough attention to the overall improvement cycle that the visit represents, including the importance of what happens before and after.

- A lack of clarity about exactly who should be learning from the rounds process and how they should be learning. Are rounds visits primarily for the benefit of the network visitors or for the host school? What, when, and how do the teachers observed on a visit learn? Since most of those who get to participate on the visit team describe it as a powerful learning opportunity, how can rounds be scaled up to provide the experience for more teachers?
- Tensions, especially in medium and large districts, between how local and how centralized aspects of the process should be. For example, a district can see the advantages of coherence and districtwide learning of having all their schools focus on the same problem of practice. On the other hand, schools that have not engaged in and have ownership of their problem of practice may end up viewing the whole process as a perfunctory compliance activity.
- The rounds practice, which cannot replace an improvement strategy and the capacity to implement it, does have a strong symbiotic relationship with it. When schools and districts have more developed improvement practices, rounds can more easily take root and accelerate them. In districts with less developed improvement practices, the rounds process can highlight the gaps.

The experience of learning about these patterns from our colleagues in the field has been both energizing and humbling. Rounds as a practice is helping to move improvement work and it is hard, slow work. We have learned to take more of a developmental mind-set about improvement—it is not "all or nothing." Schools and districts are not fixed either in the default top-down compliance culture or the engaged organizational learning culture, but move along a continuum.

The reflection on our practice and these patterns and insights have led to several important revisions in the way we teach and think about rounds and improvement. We now use a developmental approach in all aspects of the practice. We no longer frame problems of practice with questions like, "Are teachers asking higher-order thinking questions?" Instead, we asked "In what ways are teachers asking higher-order thinking questions?" as a way to move from a yes/no question to focus on the actual practice and to recognize the developmental nature of the continuum. We have learned to see pockets of improvement and to learn from them and use ideas from them to move the practice of others along the continuum.

We recognize that organizational capacity for improvement—the use of teaming, data, instructional leadership, etc.—is developmental, and we share developmental rubrics to help educators name where they are in developing the capacity. We weave the school's assessment of its improvement capacity into the next level of work discussions so the suggestions made by the visiting team can be realistic and tied to local capacity.

To help participants go below the surface in addressing the challenges that get identified during the rounds process, we do a root cause analysis like the *5 Whys* protocol. We put the problem that has been identified at the top of a piece of chart paper and ask participants to identify three to five underlying possible causes. We then look at each one in turn, again asking "Why?" and looking for the underlying causes. We continue until we have peeled away the surface issue and gotten closer to the root cause of the problem. (For a partially filled-out sample, see exhibit 1.4.) This process helps bring considerably more depth to the analysis and recommendations regarding the problem of practice that the school has identified.

We are much more explicit in teaching about and modeling adult learning. Every next-level-of-work suggestion will require some form of adult learning, since improvement can take place only with adult learning. Consequently, we work to ensure that participants have clear ideas for how adults learn, which can be woven into their follow-up suggestions.

Taken together, the insights and learning engendered by our understanding of these patterns have already led to significant improvements in the rounds practice. We are much clearer about the importance of the work before and after a visit and we use graphics like exhibit 1.2 to highlight this and to help make clear the importance of balance—of how any visit should be supporting the improvement at the host school and network level. Next-level-of-work suggestions have gotten deeper through the use of root cause analyses and are more contextually linked to the improvement structures and culture in place at the school. They have also gotten more specific about the kind of adult learning that will be necessary to help the school moved to that next level of work. This is deep cultural change work that requires teachers and administrators to think differently about learning, mind-sets, accountability, and how they work in very different ways with each for improvement.

EXHIBIT 1.4

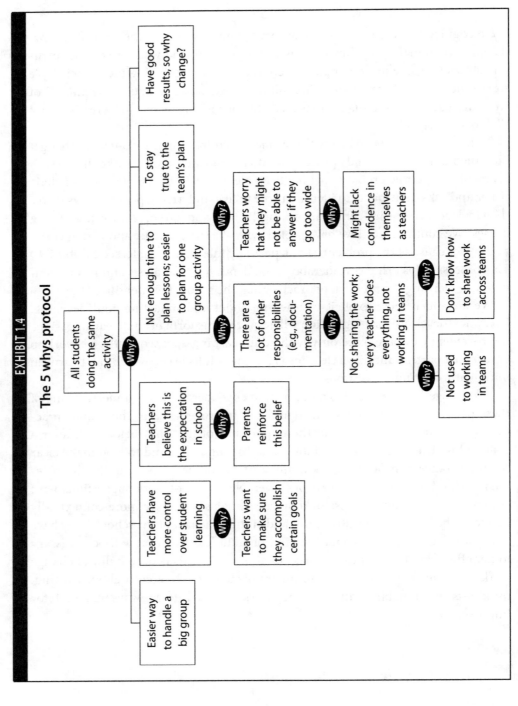

The 5 whys protocol

Note: Example developed by Stefanie Reinhorn.

Takeaways

It is in this spirit of continuous learning and improvement that we move now to look at school based rounds. School-based instructional rounds was not described in any way in *Instructional Rounds in Education*. It is an evolutionary offshoot—an example of an unanticipated innovation. What can we learn about the value of a different form of rounds? Are there ways to make suggestions through this analysis that could improve school-based rounds? Are there lessons in this work for the broader practice of cross-site instructional rounds?

Here is a set of questions to think about in reading and reacting to the next five cases, which are organized around the intersections between these school-based rounds practices and the three qualities of high-performing schools and districts:

A clear idea about what high-quality teaching and learning should look like

- How does rounds keep the focus on continuous inquiry and improvement of instruction and not just become a peer observation practice, which helps teachers share practice (a good thing) as opposed to deepen and improve it (and even better thing)? How does rounds retain a focus on all aspects of the instructional core—teachers, students, content—and not just focus on teacher behavior?
- If there is a clearly established instructional framework used in the setting, how is it used to guide rounds and help create a common focus on problems of instructional improvement without becoming so specific about classroom practices that rounds visits become implementation checks rather than continued inquiry?
- If a clearly established instructional framework is not in use, how is rounds helping to calibrate the learning of educators to help them develop common understandings of what good teaching and learning should look like in their setting?

A coherent and strategic approach to systemic improvement

- How does the rounds practice go beyond the focus on the visit to really connect with a school's continuous improvement cycle?
- Since an improvement strategy doesn't mean much unless there is the organizational capacity to enact it, how does the organizational improvement capacity of the school—its use of teams, data, instructional leadership, etc.—interact with the instructional rounds that is taking place?
- Since coherent strategy needs to exist at the school or system level and needs to be connected as a through-line to what happens in the classroom, there are two

questions worth paying attention to: How does information flow both ways, with the school or system level strategy influencing the classroom practice *and* the lessons learned in the classroom influencing the strategy? And how does the degree of local customization play out—the tensions between focusing on larger school or system issues versus more specific classroom-based practices? How can rounds help make connections between both ends of the spectrum on these two questions?

A collaborative approach to adult learning that is embedded in practice and relies on engagement and inquiry rather than compliance

- How can school-based rounds address the issues of scale—of involving more teachers as active participants—and at the same time address the role teachers are playing in rounds, specifically the question of who is learning—and how and when—from a visit?
- How does school-based rounds ensure that there is a deeper, inquiry-based approach to issues in ways that go below the surface and that incorporate a developmental mind-set, instead of a fixed or status mind-set, to the improvement efforts in the school?
- How does school-based rounds support the professionalizing of teaching and contribute to the larger culture changes that are necessary for that? This may include involving teachers and administrators in improvement work in ways that increase trust and collective efficacy and that lead to new, more lateral forms of professional accountability. It may include different ways of thinking about the relationships between teachers and administrators.

Continuing to learn about rounds and improvement

The final question does not fit under the previous headings because it cuts across all three and because it addresses a different question about how the rounds practice itself gets better. An important part of the rounds model described in *Instructional Rounds in Education: A Network Approach to Improving Teaching and Learning* is reflected in the second word in the subtitle. Cross-site rounds is a *network* practice. One of the key roles networks play is in supporting the learning of their members is helping them get the big picture of improvement, which requires making connections between all three of these, common understandings about learning and teaching, coherent strategy, and changes in the culture of how educators work together. A second is to help the participants learn from their experiences and refine and get better at the practice. Networks will typically build in periodic reflections and self-assessments, so they don't just keep "doing" rounds, but continually learn about it and improve it as a practice. School-based rounds do not have a network configuration, so a last question is:

- How do schools involved in local rounds ensure learning across a three areas and continue to learn, to grow, and to improve their rounds practice?

The goal of this chapter has been to summarize what the instructional rounds practice looks like and it what it aspires to do to improve learning and teaching in schools and professionalize the practice of education. This set of questions, drawing as it does on the big ideas and broader aspirations outlined in the chapter, provides some lenses for looking at the five cases in part 1 and lays the basis for the cross-cutting analysis in part 2. To what extent does the innovation of school-based rounds help support these larger instructional, systematic, and professionalization goals? Are there ways in which the special circumstances of school-based rounds can more effectively reach those goals? Or can some aspects of the practice actually serve to undermine them? And are there ways to take advantage of the opportunities school-based instructional rounds offers in ways that minimize the risks and losses?

CHAPTER 2

Nested Rounds in a Rural District
Killingly Memorial School

There is an air of excitement and anticipation, but also of some familiarity with an ongoing process, as the five fourth-grade teachers meet to review their protocols and focus for next week's rounds visit. "Okay, ladies, who's walking and who's being walked on?" Kate, a teacher at the school for twenty-two years, asks cheerfully. Meg smiles at the "walked on" comment—a bit of insider humor reflecting the initial anxiety many teachers felt when rounds was started two years earlier. It takes just ten minutes for the teachers to decide who will be teaching and who will be observing with the principal, the reading and special education resource teachers, and a third- and second-grade teacher. After selecting roles, the team continues to discuss the lesson plans for the day of the observation as well as the week leading up to that day. Their student data drive this conversation. Between a quarter to a third of their students are not scoring proficient on most recent state tests for fourth-graders. Kate reminds the team of the focus of this year's rounds. The fourth-grade team suspects that student tasks may not be aligned to the intent of the lesson and students may not be engaged in rigorous learning opportunities that utilize higher-order thinking. They want the observers to collect information on the Reader's Workshops that they will see to help answer two focused questions:

- *What is the intent for student learning and what is the evidence that student tasks lead to this?*
- *What are the higher-order thinking skills that students are utilizing and what is the evidence of this?*

The teachers know that on the morning of the observation the principal will meet with the members of the "walking team" for ten minutes to debrief about the protocols and what they will observe that day. It is here that they review the problem of practice that the team has chosen. Each team will observe a teacher for fifteen minutes and collect data on the specific questions, using tools that have been calibrated and shared within the school. They will spend an hour summarizing what they observed and the specific evidence they collected. After observing, the walkers will return to their other work, and at the end of the day, the fourth-grade team will reconvene to share the data and discuss what they, as a team, will do about it.

Meg still gets nervous when anyone comes into her classroom, but she is excited about the visit and what the team will learn. "It is not just a one-shot affair," she tells an observer, "but we keep cycling back to it. What we learn today will connect to what we see next week, when I get to walk and see the other half of the team. It also ties to the data team work we are doing, looking at formative assessment, and to the rounds cycle we did two months ago, working on the same problem of practice. The best part is that we know that whatever ideas we want to try out that will help us make a closer connection between rigorous student tasks and the intent of the lesson will be supported and connected to the rest of our professional development."

BACKGROUND AND CONTEXT

School-based instructional rounds in Killingly, Connecticut, grew out of a sense of frustration that the more traditional cross-site rounds practice was not really addressing the important issues. In 2008, superintendent Bill Silver, a member of the Connecticut Superintendents' Network brought the rounds practice to the district, initially for one school visit with ten of his superintendent peers, but then sustained it by providing monthly cross-school visits with principals and central office personnel within this rural, high-poverty district of five schools.

Marilyn Oat was a fourth-year principal in 2008 at Killingly Memorial School (KMS), which she describes as being the elementary school "on the poor side of town" and not as successful with its students as the teachers and she wanted. She volunteered KMS for that initial superintendent network visit and she and her teachers saw many positive aspects in Silver's decision to follow up with in-district rounds. But over the next year, they kept feeling that something was missing. "We would debrief and it felt like there was an elephant in the room," Oat says. "What wasn't being said needed to be said and what was being said was from the land of politeness." Oat and her teacher leaders asked two fundamental design questions. The first shifted the focus of rounds. instead of looking *at* the teachers, asked Oat, "What if we look *with* the teachers at the students and what they are learning? The

---

Instructional Rounds in Killingly Memorial School

- Public elementary school in a small, rural district
- Engaged in instructional rounds since 2008
- Nested rounds model (school-based rounds embedded in cross-school and cross-district rounds)
- Grade-level teams observe and debrief
- Seven- to eight-week cycle
- Anchored in districtwide focus on rigor
- Linked to improvement through lateral accountability among teachers

---

second shifted the observers and frequency of rounds: instead of having a team of outside observers visiting once every few years by the superintendent network or twice a year by administrators from within the district, what if there were much more frequent observations by teachers and others from *inside* the school?

Over the next year, with Silver's support, Oat and her team used these two design questions as a springboard for innovations of the practice. While keeping faithful to the core instructional rounds ideas of focusing on a problem of practice tied to a broader school and district theory of action, collecting specific non-judgmental data through classroom observations, and using those data to drive improvement-oriented next-level-of-work discussion, KMS added some important variations. For example, half the third-grade teachers would visit the other half one week, trade places the following week, and then use grade-level team meetings to digest findings from rounds visits and make commitments to one another about the improvements that they as a team wished to implement. The cycle was repeated every seven or eight weeks and within the first year led to quantifiable gains in the assessment metric used by the district for instructional rigor as well as subsequent gains by student on state test scores.

The focus on instructional rigor became a useful anchoring point as well as an important interim assessment for both district-based and school-based rounds in Killingly. The district's work in this area dates back to 2005–06, when, working with a team of teachers, the district developed a rigor/relevance rubric. This was initially a planning tool, but as the district developed it, the participants worked on calibrating it—watching videotapes together to see if they had a common under-standing of what rigor and relevance would look like in the classroom. The tool continued to be used for planning by teachers but also became a snapshot assess-ment done by administrators and used as a way to keep track of an important part of for district improvement.

When Killingly began to conduct district-based rounds, teachers and adminis-trators used the instrument together. So when Killingly Memorial School decided to track the changes in rigor and relevance in the classroom as an interim mea-sure in its school-based rounds, many of the teachers had already been trained on it. Using it created a strong connection to the larger district efforts. Marilyn Oat modified the form to focus only on students, removing the section of the form that looked a teacher practice (see exhibit 2.1). According to the superintendent, that was "a huge shift in changing attitudes the teachers had toward school-based rounds. So people weren't coming in and collecting data about them. They're coming to look at the kids. It took teachers out of the spotlight. Of course, anyone could see that what the kids are doing was reflective of what the teachers told them to do."

Impressed with the way the school-based rounds cycles at KMS were leading to discernible increases in instructional rigor and student learning gains, Silver directed each school in the district to develop its own version of school-based instructional rounds and has modified the use of district or cross-school rounds to better coordinate and calibrate the school-based work. He sent a clear message that not all models needed to look the same as KMS's but that all schools needed their own custom-designed school-based rounds approach.

In December 2010, Silver brought together the administrators from each of the schools to observe/participate in a KMS school-based rounds and debrief and dis-cuss it with the principal and teachers from KMS. He also asked each principal to invite a teacher leader who could play an active role in school-based rounds to join what would become a design team; he personally invited the union president, who joined the group. The day after the visit to KMS was a design day, with each school team developing its own school-based rounds.

By May 2011, the other schools in Killingly had launched school-based instruc-tional rounds. The mixed teacher/administrator design teams met two more times over the next year—once to visit and reflect on the school-based rounds model launched at the high school and again in the spring of 2012 to make refinements and calibrate their plans for growth over the coming year. When the teams came

---

EXHIBIT 2.1

Rigor rubric used in Killingly Memorial School

Results: Rigor   1   2   3   4

Rigor 4: The learning experience focuses on *deep conceptual understandings using knowledge to complete a goal* involving high-order problem-solving, decision making, investigating, inquiring, and/or creating; requires *extended engagement* in complex tasks. *Focus is on "student thinking."*

Student evidence (i.e., designing/creating; open-ended problem-solving; investigating/inquiry/decision making; developing conclusions/opinions w/ evidence or support)

☐ _____   ☐ _____
☐ _____   ☐ _____

Rigor 3: The learning experience focuses on *extending* and *refining* knowledge that promotes *conceptual understanding* of big ideas; requires a depth of reasoning about content and requires students to *think critically* outside their comfort zone; has the power to change how students "know" something. *Focus is on "student thinking."*

Student evidence (i.e., constructing responses; inductive/deductive reasoning; analyzing relevance; inquiring/hypothesizing/experimenting; comparing/contrasting; self-/peer reflecting/assessing)

☐ _____   ☐ _____
☐ _____   ☐ _____

Rigor 2: The learning experience focuses on strategies that promote factual *understanding* and/or *application* of prior knowledge and/or skills

---

Student evidence (i.e., guided practice; developing an interpretation; reading for literal comprehension; accessing/activating/applying prior knowledge; basic problem-solving; summarizing/note-taking/classifying/categorizing)

☐ _____   ☐ _____
☐ _____   ☐ _____

Rigor 1: The learning experience focuses on the *acquisition* and/or *memorization* of new information in the form of isolated, topic-related *facts* and/or *skills* with minimal connections to prior knowledge evident. Students learn and store bits of knowledge and information.

continued

EXHIBIT 2.1 *(continued)*

Student evidence (i.e., recalling/memorizing/gathering information; practicing rote skills; reading for factual information; passively receiving information)

☐ _____   ☐ _____
☐ _____   ☐ _____

Source: Adapted with permission from William Silver, Superintendent of Schools, Killingly Public Schools, Connecticut.

together, they not only shared their ideas and models for school-based rounds and gave and received feedback on them, but they also talked collectively with central office staff about how the district-based rounds needed to change to best support and complement the school-based versions that were going on in each school.

THE PRACTICE

Before the Visit

Because of the district's focus on rigor and critical literacy, in a broad sense all the problems of practice in Killingly are about those twin ideas. However, Killingly has always embraced some local variation—customization of the problem of practice to focus on issues of concern at the local school level. Finding the balance between this "local twist" and staying connected to a broader strategy has been a critical challenge. According to Bill Silver, principals like Marilyn Oat help the teachers customize the work further (i.e., to their grade-level teams) and also help them see how all the pieces fit together, but exactly how this is done, and how well it is done varies substantially across the different schools. At Killingly Memorial School, the team leaders come in during the summer and, after reviewing test scores and other data, come up with the problem of practice for the school. Then it gets customized further for each grade-level team—as in "What does this focus mean for K or first grade—what are we working on around this problem of practice?"

In the first year, the school-based rounds were only conducted at each grade level. After the early experience of teacher discomfort with making comments and giving feedback about their peers, Oat switched the focus to be on the students and on what they were learning. She literally took the role of the teacher off of the observation form, leaving only the focus on the task and the role of the student. After a successful first year, with teachers feeling both comfortable about the observations and pleased that the tracking of the rigor in the classroom showed an upward trend, teachers were encouraged to think more "vertically"—about the whole school. A visit to the third-grade team, for example, might include a second- and fourth-grade teacher. Lisa Higgins, a third-grade teacher leader involved in rounds work from the outset, describes this process: "We got better with it and the whole idea of the vertical alignment. When we only did our grade level, we didn't pay as much attention to what the students were coming with, and what the next-grade-level teachers were expecting. When we started the vertical alignment, we shifted to 'This is the expectation of where we want our third-graders to come in, and this where we want them at the end of the year.'" By the third year, teams were also starting to disaggregate data by looking at differences based on gender, free or reduced-price lunch eligibility, and special education status as ways to fine-tune how their teaching reached all students.

Within that overall framing, the specific focus for a particular visit cycle is planned by the team that would be observed. The teachers agree on a common intent for the lesson, use that to identify specific practices that teachers will be using to reach that goal, and then focus the observations on those practices.

At the Visit

Rounds at KMS are conducted once a week, rotating through the grade levels, creating a roughly two-month cycle. Half the teachers on a grade level, accompanied by the principal, specialists, unified arts teachers, and more recently, a teacher from the grade above and one from the grade below, observe the other half, and then flip the following week (see exhibit 2.2). Teachers who are observing (typically five for each visit) have substitute coverage for their classes, drawing on a stable pool of subs used by the school. They divide into two teams of three or four and spend fifteen to twenty minutes in each of the three classrooms.

As observers, teachers are expected to remain focused on evidence of student work, use calibrated instruments on rigor, and to be nonjudgmental of teacher practices. Visits and discussions are expected to be tightly tied to use of protocols, many of which are modified versions of the instructional rounds practice. Teachers are also expected to "steal ideas" as they observe.

Officially the visits are facilitated by the principal or by teacher leaders. Because Marilyn Oat sees the rounds as so central to her role in helping the school continue to improve, she ends up participating in all of them, at all grade levels. When asked by fellow principals about how she can take so much time for rounds off from her

---

EXHIBIT 2.2

Sample problem of practice and schedule:
Killingly Memorial School, Grade 4

Theory of action:

If students are engaged in rigorous learning opportunities utilizing higher-order thinking in language arts then student achievement will increase.

Problem of practice:

23.1% of our current Grade 4 students did not achieve proficiency in reading as measured by their 2010–2011 CMT. 34.1% of our Grade 4 students did not achieve proficiency in reading as measured by the DRA in May 2011. Student tasks may not be aligned to the intent of the lesson. Students may not be engaged in rigorous learning opportunities that utilize higher-order thinking.

Questions for focus:

What is the intent for student learning? Do student tasks lead to the intent for student learning? To what degree are students involved in higher-order thinking?

	Group A	Group B
11:00–11:10	Meet in Room 301. Establish protocols.	
11:10–11:35	K— Room XXX	M— Room XXX
11:35–12:05	Room XXX	Room XXX
12:05–1:15	Walk-thru team Debrief in Conference Room	
1:15–1:45	Lunch	
1:45–3:00	Grade-level/whole-team debrief Conference Room	

Walk-thru teams:

A. Joe Musumeci
   Joan Burlingame
   Lisa Higgins

B. Marilyn Oat
   Liz Amburn
   Janice Joly
   Marcia Griffiths-Farquhar

Source: Adapted with permission from William Silver, Superintendent of Schools, Killingly Public Schools, Connecticut.

other work, Oat says simply, "This *is* my work. The time I spend with teachers looking at and asking questions about instruction—that is the work of a principal." Lisa Higgins, who works closely with Oat, notes that the frequent rounds visits also provide the principal with substantial regular interaction with the students, allowing her to really know who the children are and what they are learning.

While the general sequence of the instructional rounds practice is adhered to at KMS, the school has customized the protocols in some significant ways to better meet their improvement approach and to take advantage of the *school-based* nature of the practice:

- The focus on students rather than teachers, which started as a way to defuse teacher concerns about being having their teaching "judged" by others, has taken on a different meaning in a school-based setting. Unlike in a cross-school visit, the teachers observing actually know the students, the curriculum content, or both quite intimately. In some cases, the students have been taught by the observing teacher in another grade; in others, grade-level teacher peers are observing a lesson that their team helped plan and that they are teaching in their own classrooms. During these visits, substantial time is spent in close observation and discussion with students and the level of questioning of students on content is much higher and more detailed than in a typical cross-school visit.
- The sticky notes and affinity protocol that are used in most rounds visits are replaced by having observers write directly on a customized recording form (see exhibit 2.3). These are used throughout the day to gather data, create patterns, predictions, and next level of work. They are shredded at the end of the day.
- After the observation, the debriefing team sits together for an hour, summarizing:
  □ Intent of the lesson
  □ Evidence
  □ Prediction: If you were a student in this class . . .
  □ What does rigor look like here
  □ What are we going to steal
  □ What is next level of work

The observers then go around the room to share what they saw and recorded in each class, focusing on one teacher at a time. The principal records and compiles their responses onto one sheet to share with the teachers, who would hear the

EXHIBIT 2.3

Killingly Memorial School observation form

Teacher rounds

An opportunity for teachers to observe, collaborate, and reflect

Teacher observed _____   Time _____

Key questions
- What is the intent for student learning?
- To what degree are the students involved or engaged in higher-order thinking?

Classify the rigor of the tasks students are performing . . . *Recalling, identifying, inferring, demonstrating, investigating, critiquing, evaluating, creating*	*Intent of student learning:* *Reader's workshop: How critically are students thinking and engaged in the mini-lesson?*
	Student task *Record what you observe the students doing . . .*

Source: Adapted with permission from William Silver, Superintendent of Schools, Killingly Public Schools, Connecticut.

summary later in the day when the observed teachers joined the observers (see a partial sample of this record in exhibit 2.4). At the end of the day, after the feedback has been shared, the team (observers and teachers who have been observed) discuss the next-level-of-work suggestions. Rather than these being made by outsiders who would then be leaving, they are made by the grade-level teachers themselves. Essentially they are identifying their next level of work, to which they are committing as a team. According to Oat, this is when the real discussion and learning takes place: "They talk about the impact, the implications and where they need to learn and grow."

EXHIBIT 2.4

Partial sample of Killingly Memorial School recording form

Walkthrough debriefing

Grade: 4

Observers:	*Teaching teachers:*
Lisa Higgins/ G3	K—
Liz Amburn	M—
Joan Burlingame	
Janice Joly	
Marcia Griffiths-Farquhar	
Joe Musumeci	
Marilyn Oat	

- How was the intent of the lesson evidenced in student task/s? What can we expect students to do as a result of this learning?
  Intent: *Ability to summarize; ability to sequence*
  Evidence: *Great discussion as to what this might look like.*

- What did rigor look like?
  Discussion around academic rigor and social behavior rigor. Team has questions regarding what rigor looks like in reader's workshop and will explore this. Social/Behavior rigor that was evidenced included time on task, student engagement and student partnerships.

- Other observations—effective teaching practices:
  Modeling: *Active and with movement*
  Charts regarding listener and reteller behavior/expectations
  Current "conversation" re books in that they related to student's schema
  Book choice

continued

EXHIBIT 2.4 *(continued)*

- As observers, what did we learn? What are our questions? What would we like to "steal"?

  Learned: *We are confused! Conversation regarding retelling vs summarizing.*

  Questions: *Could students speak to what was a main event?*

  Was "retelling" (i.e., "taking big steps in time") new learning?

  Do our students know they have been retelling since kindergarten?

  (Retelling: Refer to Lucy Calkins, vol 1, p. 222—Retelling is considered a lower-order thinking skill) Should we be teaching both skills, retelling and use either retelling or summarizing—depending on audience and purpose?

  Question: *I wonder if having a team intent will work in reader's workshop?*

  Was the whole group lesson a mini-lesson?

  Steal: "How will We Spend Our Time Today" chart

- Do we see patterns?

  Students not clear about "purpose" regarding their independent reading.

- What is the next level of work?

  Better understanding/communication of retelling versus summary (are we teaching to the DRA?)

  Clarify vocabulary K–4 regarding retelling vs summary and expectations at each level.

  Book study: "Choice Words"

Source: Adapted with permission from William Silver, Superintendent of Schools, Killingly Public Schools, Connecticut.

After the Visit

The follow-up from the visit can be thought of at team, school, and district level, although arguably the most powerful impacts are at the team level.

Team.   Every part of the visit is tightly tied to the grade-level team. The visit debriefs flow right into the team's weekly planning meeting, so even though rounds is on a seven- or eight-week cycle, there is no delay before teachers can begin implementing the next-level-of-work suggestions they have decided on. Developing high-functioning teams has been a priority at KMS at least since 2008, when the school worked on developing data teams with Connecticut's State Education Resource Center (SERC).

Lisa Higgins describes the learning process: "When we first started this, you always had a team that got it faster and more efficiently than others. Because of the work with data teams, the school was comfortable with use of videotaping and sharing between teams. We focused on making sure teams were asking probing questions, getting participation from everyone, and holding each other accountable." Because of the common experience with working on calibrating rigor in classrooms, it was a relatively easy transition to helping team leaders identify what rigor in a team meeting needs to look like. Teams would be videotaped during meetings and other teams would watch. In addition, in keeping with focusing on the "vertical," more schoolwide focus, Higgins adds, "We would also share things from one team to another. When rubrics were developed for a grade level, they got passed up to the next grade, so you knew the expectation from each grade level and how that changed from year to year."

When, after a visit, agreements and commitments are made at the grade-level team meeting, particularly focused on what teachers will be doing differently in the classrooms, there is a clear expectation that the school-based team will be looking for particular instructional actions during its next visit. This form of lateral accountability has been both a powerful lever for change and improvement—having your colleagues back to see if you are doing what you all agreed to do—and it has also led to questions from teachers about how to work with reluctant colleagues. Margaret Walker, a fourth-grade team leader involved in rounds from its beginning, tells a story that captures the powerful interplay between teacher-to-teacher communication, follow-up expectations, and teacher accountability. The events she describes took place after one of the district's instructional rounds visits (which brought in administrators from central office and other schools):

> A few people on the team went off and did something different than planned. We all said we were going to teach X, and some people did Y. It led to a challenging conversation for us teachers to have. "Why did people do that?" members of the team wondered. The team was hurt, and saying, "'If [the lesson we had planned] wasn't good enough and you felt like you could add something, why didn't you say so?" And it's about our accountability and how we work together. How, as we are moving forward, can we have more successful relationships on our team so that everyone feels heard about how they want to teach a particular lesson? And if we agree on something . . . You realize that rounds opens things up to see when people follow through and when they don't. It was a hard conversation, but we actually had more camaraderie on the team as a result.

Teacher leader Higgins tells a similar story that highlights the change in ownership among teachers when the lateral accountability is high:

> We have a district walkthrough coming up this week. The whole district is coming to a building. And we all get that angst again. For our team specifically, it didn't go

well last year, since there were those outliers who did what they wanted to do versus what the team had decided to do. They were the first ones this year to say, "We have to sit down as a team and we've really got to talk about this. And we need to make sure that we are all moving in the same direction."

Schoolwide. In larger faculty meetings, the data from the individual visits are posted and used to connect with and generate schoolwide learning. In the first year, Oat kept a scatterplot that reported out the levels of rigor in the classrooms in the different grade levels, and made that available for people to see the growth in rigor over time. In addition, in the last year, the notes from a given visit are left posted in the room that all the teams meet in so people can see what others are working on. There is a place for teachers from other grade levels to look at the notes and to post questions for the other teams. Sharing the data and inviting questions from different grade-level teams help support vertical alignment and reduce the gaps that often show up between grade levels; for instance, where the fourth-grade teachers might otherwise be blaming the third-grade teachers for not having sufficiently prepared the students (see exhibit 2.5). Nonetheless, this is still a work in progress, with Oat not only inviting questions from teachers on other grade levels, but inviting them on visits to see for themselves. Team leader Margaret Walker sees these as important efforts but also notes, "We are moving in the direction of working schoolwide—the vertical piece. But we haven't gotten there yet. We are still pretty compartmentalized. I am not sure if it's the structure of the day, or the layout of the building—I can go for long periods of time without really seeing somebody from the primary grade levels—or if it's the overall school culture in our district."

District. Superintendent Bill Silver notes that, although there are elements of the follow-up after rounds visit that are looser than he would like, there are several important connections between the school-based rounds visits and the district work. The lessons and experiences of the school-based rounds visits become grist for conversations with the superintendent and deputy superintendent, as well as for their supervisory meetings with principals. And just as rigor and relevance gave people a common language, so do the language and practices of rounds. Silver notices that even in a small district, the variation between what rounds looks like and what kind of impact it seems to be having at the different schools is very high. He notes that some visits seemed more as if they were for show; as he puts it, "People knew how to use the words, but the depth of the conversation was not there." Silver looks for movement out of the "land of nice" as a way of tracking

EXHIBIT 2.5

A guide to higher-order questioning and thinking

In order to help our student think at deeper levels—beyond information presented on the printed page—and critically analyze information presented, this guide is being created. It is a starting place and is meant to be a catalyst for us, as teachers, as we strive to become more critically literate in our questioning skills.

Please use the attached pages to add ideas and suggestions from your grade level. Thank you!

Sample questions/ideas:

- Why? Why? Why? Explain. Explain. Explain. Show evidence . . .
- Asking students to look at motives, causes, and relationships . . .
- Asking students to put information together in a different way by combining elements in a new pattern or proposing a different solution.
- Asking students to present and defend an opinion or make a judgment based on a set of criteria.
- What inference can you make? Support evidence from text.
- What conclusions can you draw? What makes you believe this?
- What evidence can you find to support your answer?
- How would another character tell this story? Why? Explain.
- Who is in the story/picture? Who is missing? Explain your thoughts.
- Can you predict the outcome? What makes you believe this?
- Do you agree with . . . ? Why or why not?
- How would you prioritize? Why?
- Score your writing and explain your score showing evidence.
- What are the intentions of the author? What does the author want the reader to think?
- Whose voices are represented? Whose voices are marginalized or discounted?
- How does the story change when you replace key characters with people of the opposite gender?
- Tell the story in a different setting? How would it change the story?

Rigor: What does it look like? What have we learned?

Kindergarten
- Identify fiction/nonfiction and explain.
- Making predictions and explaining why with evidence from the text.

continued

EXHIBIT 2.5 *(continued)*

- Cause and effect . . . If you do this, what will happen next . . .?
- Making inferences from pictures in a story . . .
- Would you like this character as a friend? Why or why not?
- Compare/contrast the letter "a" and "b" . . . How are they the same? How are they different?

Grade 1
- When students were cognizant of why they chose the strategy that they did and could explain why.
- Decision making—weighing options/choices.
- Reflecting—students were able to share what the liked best, listen and ask pertinent questions.
- Students noting same/different in making connections at more than a superficial level.
- Student ability to verbalize strategies and share how they helped them as readers. How did you know that this strategy as helpful?
- Students sharing what they were confused by and determining if it was a content or word confusion.
- "I'm thinking Annie's in trouble. Why?"—justifying.
- Self and peer assessing and reflecting on why.

Grade 2
- Comparing ideas about important events and explaining why.
- Comparing important and not important parts of the story and telling why.
- Giving the character in a story advice and explaining why.
- Looking for a change in the character—noting before/after or compare/contrast.
- Proving connections by sharing evidence from the text.
- Analyzing T/T, T/W, T/S by going deeper than surface connections—bringing in feelings.
- The ability to distinguish between important and not important and explain why.
- Reading a story and being able to support our choice of author's message with evidence from the text.
- Student evaluating and judging characters to determine traits.
- Evaluating and deciding if student would want character as a friend and explaining why.

progress that the different schools are having toward deeper conversations about school improvement.

He also notes that the district has not been explicit enough in connecting the rounds work—whether school- or district-based—to each school's school improvement plan and the reports given by the principals to the district data team. He views this as a next level of work for the district. Even though the individual school improvement plans were built around rounds, when the principals would come in and talk about their work, sometimes they would not make any mention of the rounds, so "they weren't using rounds in their efforts on implementing the scope of work other than saying we're doing rounds."

NESTED ROUNDS—SCHOOL-BASED ROUNDS IN A LARGER SYSTEM OF ROUNDS

Throughout the process of going to scale—moving from having one school engaged in school-based rounds to having all of them involved—Superintendent Silver was always clear that district-based rounds would continue, but might be modified to better complement the school-based work, and might be reduced in frequency so educators would not be "rounded" out. (In fact, the frequency was reduced from ten per year (two per school) when it started, to five per year.) As school-based rounds ramped up in Killingly, district-based (cross-school) rounds evolved to be focused on making sure the relative isolation of school-based rounds didn't undercut the school and district improvement efforts. One purpose was calibration—to make sure observers were consistent in how they assessed rigor on a district-developed instrument and to assure that core principles of rounds were being applied with fidelity to the model. Another goal was to make sure that outside perspectives and ideas regularly came into each school, to help with school learning and prevent the kind of egg-crate isolation that can stymie school improvement efforts. A key part of this philosophy is that outsiders also often notice things that insiders miss.

To help all these processes work well together, Killingly developed a form of *nested rounds*—where the school-based rounds take place in a larger system of rounds. In its second year of school- and district-based rounds, Killingly organized itself so that the school-based rounds were scheduled first, so the district visits could be piggybacked onto existing school-based rounds. That way, the district rounds looks like an expanded version of school-based rounds, and then the rare event of the superintendent's rounds could be built around that as well. This also enables principals to think strategically about when to use the outsiders to provide additional feedback or otherwise enhance a visit.

A key part of thinking about nested rounds has been the goal of ensuring that school system learning and school-to-school learning were taking place in ways that would contribute to coherence and not lead to fragmentation. This aspect is enhanced by having system leaders on these visits paying particular attention to what are some of the common issues that are showing up across the schools. It also reminds schools of their interdependence—that they are part of one system—and enables educators in one school to see what is happening with their prospective students or with their graduates by looking at other points in the system (e.g., elementary, middle, high school). The Killingly district has also tried to reach the same goal by posting the school-based rounds schedule for each of the schools in the beginning of the school year and then encouraging schools to cross over and create some vertical connections in the district. For example, staff from the Good-year Early Childhood Center have participated in rounds at the elementary school and vice versa, although this is still more of an isolated event than an organized pattern.

CONNECTION TO INSTRUCTIONAL IMPROVEMENT AND THEORIES OF LEARNING FOR ADULTS

Silver notes the strong connection between school-based rounds and his theory of action for overall district improvement: "The whole thing about school-based rounds is the direct involvement of teachers and the professionalization of the role. That's where I think the whole power of school-based rounds is, as opposed to district or network rounds. It is because teachers are the ones that are observing each other and hopefully are becoming honest with each other, and need to be self-reflective enough so they can hear the messages so that they can adjust their instruction accordingly. It's a huge investment of time on everybody's part—administrators and teachers—so there has to be enough value in it."

For years, Silver had seen educators in the district go to conferences and learn new ideas, but there was a gap between the knowing and the doing. In his view, "People would seem to understand the literature about an idea, but were not necessarily implementing it. Rounds became a tool that linked the knowing and doing, in part because it forced principals to be in classrooms to see what was going on instead of taking teachers' word for was going on."

For Marilyn Oat, rounds was the perfect complement to her idea of how adults learn and improve: "My job as principal is to ask questions, and to keep inquiry going. I am the chief questioner—that is how I help our teachers learn."

ASSESSING IMPACTS AND EVOLVING THE ROUNDS PRACTICE

Killingly Memorial School has kept track of both quantitative impact measures and qualitative ones. In addition to tracking the numeric scores on the district's rigor and relevance instrument, it uses student test score data from internal, formative assessments. These mostly teacher-made tests, based on a completed unit, are then tracked and correlated with the more summative Connecticut Mastery Test. The gains seen on each of these measures—rigor scores, formative tests, and the state exam—have all helped reinforce the positive improvement cycle at KMS.

Participants also note important qualitative changes—impacts on changes in culture for teams, teachers, and students as well as impacts on individual teachers.

Team leader Margaret Walker describes the impact of rounds on teamwork and the consistency of instruction among the teachers on a team:

> Rounds gave us the push to have open and honest conversations with each other: "Let's see what teacher A, who has better results in her classroom, has done and see what we can learn from it." Rounds has led to greater consistency. So now, when you are on an observation, if you go into see a lesson in one of the teacher's rooms, and then go into see another teacher's room it's almost like the lesson is continuing. It is not exactly the same, because all of us are different people. But you can see the idea and the concept of the lesson being taught, and you can actually see the progression of that lesson across classrooms as you move in a walk.

Lisa Higgins talks about the impact on the teachers and on the students:

> Personally I always left those observations thinking, "Wow, I really could be doing that," or going back and rethinking things I was doing in my own classroom to make them better. The kids would have a substitute for the day, and I always presented the rounds visits to the students as part of the learning process for us as teachers, saying, "This is what I'm going out to do, and next time it will be our turn for people to come and see what we're doing." When I would come back into the classroom, I would approach things by saying "When I was in this other class, this is what I saw, and we need to change how we are doing this, because I think it worked better." or "Hey, I learned this—let's try it." I found that when the kids are part of that process, there is just an excitement about them also being the experts when someone comes into your room. That they have a job—to show those teachers what they're doing. This was especially true when we changed to have people coming in looking at the students, because people were much more engaged with the students, not just sitting and watching the teachers. The kids need to be part of that process—they need

almost that to see this as a kind of "professional development" for them: "What does this look like, what does it mean, and what can it do for me?"

Walker makes a similar connection to the learning for her students: "When presented effectively, rounds meets the innate need to know about what is going on next door. It helps us satisfy that curiosity, and not just the teachers but for students. And when they are asked questions during a visit, the kids feel valued and that they are contributing to the learning in the school and they also learn about the feedback—'What did they say about us?'"

Walker also notes the teachers are more likely to take risks and try new innovations in their own classroom, especially if they have planned their lessons together as part of the team. And Higgins adds how the accountability piece—seeing the different levels of success each teacher had with the same curriculum—encourages the learning from one another: "One of the teachers on my team, who was extremely reluctant to be observed last year, asked to be first one observed this year. She said, 'I know that I need to get better, because I wasn't doing what you all were doing. And I want my kids to have what your kids have. ' That's huge, and I'm not so sure that that would happen if we weren't going into each other's rooms."

Principal Oat tells a powerful story about a thirty-five-year veteran whom she had spent some years trying to encourage to leave, whose teaching experience has been transformed by participating in rounds: "She has turned around. She is now asking the questions of herself, of her teaching, always looking for data and ways to see impacts on students and support her continued learning. Her team now says 'wow' and now I look at her and said 'No, you can't leave.'"

Grade 3

- Identify traits—provide evidence to support.
- Determining importance.
- Validating predictions within their personal text.
- Putting yourself in the character's shoes and how you would evaluate this character.
- Stretching out predictions: supporting and explaining why.
- Justify by giving proof and information that led the student to reach their decision.
- Self reflection in the use of a rubric.
- Evaluating/judging—deciding important information to share as listeners evaluate whether information is sufficient.
- Conversations between students where they analyzed what they felt was important and what was not important.
- Comparing and contrasting characters.
- Making inferences, judgments about characters using evidence from text as support.
- In developing a summary, students had to make judgments/decisions regarding important information regarding the beginning, middle, end of a story.

Grade 4

Asking students to "prove," justify their answer (even in decoding/skill work).

- Showing evidence from text to support your answer.
- Metacognition . . . self awareness of reading behaviors—student self-evaluating.
- Evaluating/analyzing—use of think-marks.
- Students verbally comparing and contrasting characters as protagonist and/or antagonist in small groups and on a graphic organizer.
- Students describing/explaining how a character's beliefs guided their actions in a whole group setting.
- Students identifying the most surprising event and making a text-to-text connection.
- Students identifying the emotions of characters associated with the adversity they were facing.
- Students labeling/scoring a response to a guided question and explaining why.

Source: Adapted with permission from William Silver, Superintendent of Schools, Killingly Public Schools, Connecticut.

CHAPTER 3

Stand-Alone Rounds in a K–12 Urban Charter School
Pegasus School of Liberal Arts and Sciences

"It works! It really works," Virginia Hart told her companions with more than a little excitement creeping into her voice. She was with Frances Teran and Virginia Lannen, the assistant CEO and CEO, respectively, of the Pegasus Charter School leadership team. They were wrapping up a weekly leadership meeting off campus when Virginia got the news from the rounds team: "Their observations on Tuesday showed a measurable increase in the numbers of teachers using academic language—and even increases in the number students using it too."

It was the first revisit, using a repeat of a problem of practice, since Pegasus had moved to a new team structure for supporting teaching a few months earlier and to a new approach to using instructional rounds to support improvement. As the Coordinator for Curriculum, Instruction, and Initiatives, Virginia had been working for over a year to convince her leadership colleagues that short-cycle, tightly focused rounds visits would be the best way to leverage improvement at the school. And here was the payoff. For several months now, the problems of practice had been tight and narrowly focused. The team leaders in the new structure had conducted the rounds, developed patterns and predictions, and then planned and delivered several weeks of professional development to improve what was going on in the classrooms.

And then this. "It took longer to get here than I thought it would," Virginia said. "Here it is December and we are first cycling back to look at this problem of practice on academic language that we first did at a rounds visit on in October. But there were workshops every week on it for four weeks, and look at the results!"

"I am thrilled that we are seeing a strong payoff for the work that is being done," said CEO Lannen.

"I agree," said Teran. "The team leaders can go back and say 'We organized and delivered those trainings, and now we can see how they lead to improvements in the classroom.'"

Virginia Hart smiled as she reminded her colleagues about how some of those team leaders had complained about the narrow focus and the repetition. "They would almost get bored, saying, 'This is the third time I am observing vocabulary usage this semester.' I told them, 'If our end goal is that almost all of our students are comfortable with this vocabulary usage, until you can answer the question about how much our students are using academic language in their literacy work, we are going to keep doing it.' Repetition of that narrow focus, in the long run, is much better. A broad focus would be less measurable and we would have trouble seeing improvement."

"So this is great," Virginia Lannen tells her colleagues. "It will help us keep our improvement work and our rounds work moving. After today, the team leaders—everyone—they can all appreciate the tangible benefits of their work on this."

BACKGROUND AND CONTEXT

The Pegasus School of Liberal Arts and Sciences is a K–12 charter school in downtown Dallas, serving an ethnically diverse group of 662 students, three-quarters of whom qualify for free or reduced-price lunch. The teachers are a mix of a relatively small, stable group of long-term faculty members and a larger group of newer, less experienced staff, many of whom teach for a few years and then leave, often to traditional districts after completing state certification requirements while at Pegasus. As a freestanding charter school, Pegasus only engages in instructional rounds internally. (There reportedly is another charter school in the area conducting rounds but no connections have yet been made to it.) Pegasus began its involvement with instructional rounds in 2009 after reading about rounds in *Instructional Rounds in Education*. Since then, its evolution with rounds has gone through three phases.

At the beginning, in 2009, Pegasus organized rounds by departments, and its experience for the first year was positive, largely because people were getting into teachers' classrooms and observing practice. People felt stuck, however, when it came to the next level of work, and also found that having problems of practice focused at the departmental level ended up leading to a certain amount of defensiveness, thus reducing the learning. After attending a Rounds Institute at Harvard

---

Instructional Rounds in Pegasus School of Liberal Arts and Sciences

- K–12 charter school in urban setting
- Engaged in instructional rounds since 2009
- Stand-alone rounds model
- Teacher leaders and school administrators observe and debrief
- Three-week cycle
- Anchored in school's theory of action
- Linked to improvement through professional development

Graduate School of Education and shifting to more of a schoolwide problem of practice for the next two years, leaders of the school felt that they had gotten better at doing rounds and sharing practice in this second phase, but were still not as successful at getting substantial instructional improvement from the work.

In the spring of 2012, the Pegasus team attended a second Institute (Instructional Rounds 2, designed specifically for schools and school districts that had been involved in rounds for at least one year). When they returned for what they think of as "phase 3," they not only changed the rounds practice, but they changed the way their school was organized. To get greater impacts, they divided the sixty-five teachers in the school into thirteen cadres composed of three teachers who would work with approximately sixty students for two years. They created positions for five cadre leaders—experienced teachers who would provide oversight and support for two or three cadres apiece. These five teachers have reduced teaching schedules that enable them to participate in rounds and related activities all day every Tuesday. They also take lead responsibility for planning and implementing the weekly staff development sessions that take place after the students leave early on each Wednesday. Along with the school director, the cadre leaders compose the rounds visiting team. (There has been some discussion of inviting other teachers on rounds in the future, but that has not yet been done.)

Every Tuesday, the rounds team divides into three groups of two to visit classrooms, focusing on a problem of practice agreed on at the beginning of the school year. They do not try to visit every classroom every week, but do visit three classrooms, deliberately set up to be in different subject areas, during each observation cycle. The subject areas and the teachers are varied with each round cycle. Virginia Hart, District Coordinator for Curriculum, Instruction, and Initiatives, oversees the rounds and professional development for the school. She organizes each of the round cycles, helps develop and tune the problems of practice, and is available as a resource for the rounds team, although she does not routinely attend each one.

The three-week cycles in the current phase (phase 3) are organized as follows:

- *Week 1:* This is a time for observation of three classrooms, followed by patterns and predictions.
- *Week 2:* The team has most of the day blocked off to dig more deeply into the root causes of the patterns and predictions that seem most important, using the 5 Whys protocol to help get to a root cause analysis. It also has a formal meeting at the end of Tuesday that addresses some of the administrative work that the cadre leaders and the school director face together: paperwork and documentation of teachers, lesson plans, field trip plans, status updates on where everyone stands on yearlong requirements, etc.
- *Week 3:* The rounds team is in charge of training sessions that are held on Wednesdays for teacher professional development (students leave early on Wednesdays). It takes the insights from the patterns and predictions and from the 5 Whys to plan and deliver the next three Wednesdays' professional development sessions. This is an ongoing cycle, with a connection between the Tuesday observation and the patterns that are used to plan the Wednesday professional development cycle, even as the next round of Tuesday observations is moving forward.

THE PRACTICE

Before the Visit

During the first year, problems of practice were developed at the departmental level and departmental leaders went on the visits in their departments. That created difficulties, according to Virginia Hart, because some of the department leaders got very defensive—"way too defensive to improve from." In years two and three, Pegasus moved to a whole school problem of practice, which helped defuse the tension. Hart also tried to set up the observation schedule to minimize the amount of time a department leader would be observing his or her own department. But the focus of the problems of practice was still broad. Virginia Lannen, Pegasus's chief executive officer, notes that in the early years, she contributed to that perspective. She wanted the problem of practice to "help the school achieve immediate perfection." After attending the Rounds 2 Institute in spring 2012, she has changed her outlook: "I wanted them to do too much. I wanted everything to be done immediately. The big change that Virginia Hart implemented this year was to really limit what we were looking at, so we are able to have major improvement in a smaller context."

Problem of practice development at Pegasus is tightly linked to the school's stated theory of action. Consistent with the shift described in CEO Lannen's comment, both have gotten more tightly focused on classroom practices. Pegasus uses the summer to come up with the problems of practice that it will be focusing on for each team. The problems of practice are specifically tied to one of the three elements of the school's theory of action. For example, part of its theory of action last year read: *If students are able to think critically, to express themselves clearly, and apply this knowledge outside the classroom, then they will be high-achieving students who are ready for college and career.* One of the two problems of practice tied to this portion of the theory of action would be:

> #1: *Students are dependent solely on support materials and teachers rather than drawing their own conclusions from their experiences and knowledge base. What are the students doing? How are teachers scaffolding student learning? Are teachers asking didactic questions? To what extent are students referring to prior knowledge when faced with new problems addressing similar objectives?*

See exhibit 3.1 to see other problems of practice associated with this theory of action and other theories and linked problems of practice.

Pegasus has more narrowly and specifically focused both its theories of action around improvement and the problems of practice that are associated with them. For example, now in its fourth year of rounds, part of the school's theory of action is: *If students use proper vocabulary in each of their respective classes, are required to communicate in proper English, and if students have structured reading time in every class, then their literacy skill will improve.* One of the two problems of practice used for this would be:

> #1: *Our students have trouble comprehending academic information and successfully using the information the students have received, through reading or other activities, to complete assigned work and process and apply the*

EXHIBIT 3.1

Year 3 theories of action and related problems of practice

Theory of action 1

If students are able to think critically, to express themselves clearly, and apply this knowledge outside the classroom, then they will be high-achieving students who are ready for college and career.

Linked problems of practice:

#1: Students are dependent solely on support materials and teachers rather than drawing their own conclusions from their experiences and knowledge base. What are the students doing? How are teachers scaffolding student learning? Are teachers asking didactic questions? To what extent are students referring to prior knowledge when faced with new problems addressing similar objectives?

#2: Students learn content specifics without application. Are students only learning discipline or unit specific skills and processes or are they learning concepts that may be applied?

Theory of action 2

If teachers build a fun and nonthreatening environment where students feel free to ask questions, share opinions to take academic risks, then student engagement and knowledge retention will improve.

Linked problems of practice:

#1: Students do not often verbally participate when they are in class. It is difficult to know if they understand what is going on in the class. How does the teacher invite participation from all students? To what extent does the task elicit participation from the students?

#2: Students are hesitant to speak up in classes that they are weak in. They often sit quietly in class and shy away from being called on or volunteering for answers. What type of body language is evident from the students that may reflect feelings of fear, hesitancy, or apprehension? What opportunities are given to the students that allow them to participate within class discussions?

Theory of action 3

If we develop a culture of accountability and respect for the school and the community, then students will value and practice high academic achievement and community responsibility.

Linked problem of practice:

#1:   Students at Pegasus want an atmosphere of respect when they attend class. Even though etiquette, citizenship and conflict resolution are a part of our curriculum, students continue to need guidance. To what extent do the tasks students are being asked to do provide opportunities to practice respect in the classroom? What are the different ways in which students are showing respect and disrespect in the classroom? How are the rules and expectations communicated to the students? Is there evidence that students understand and are following rules and expectations of the classroom?

Source: Adapted with permission from Virginia Lannen, CEO, Pegasus School of Liberal Arts and Sciences, Dallas, Texas.

> *information learned on higher than a remembering level because the students do not understand the vocabulary necessary to be successful in their academic classes.*

What strategies are teachers using to help students learn academic vocabulary and use the vocabulary in class?

For other examples of how Pegasus's theories of action and problems of practice are more narrow and specific in year four, see exhibit 3.2.

At the beginning of the year, during teacher training, teachers learn about what the rounds process is, why Pegasus thinks it is valuable to school improvement, how it differs from formal observations, and how the teachers will help in the process.

At the Visit

According to Hart, the hard part of adapting to a visit inside of a school, as opposed to cross-school rounds, is that "you know the people—and sometimes you know them well. So it becomes hard to keep it on a professional level and to protect the anonymity. It can become easy just to skip ahead [on the protocol] and say, 'Oh, let's just do this.' You really have to work on staying with the process." She goes on to note that the visitors always spend thirty minutes in each classroom, but

> the debate is always about being only in half of a class and "Perhaps we just didn't see this" or "I read their lesson plans, and they may have done this last week and we just didn't see it." I would reiterate that if you don't see it in the half the class that you've

---

EXHIBIT 3.2

Year 4 theories of action and related problems of practice

Theory of action 1

If students use proper vocabulary in each of their respective classes, are required to communicate in proper English, and if students have structured reading time in every class, then their literacy skill will improve.

Linked problems of practice:

#1: Our students have trouble comprehending academic information and successfully using the information the students have received, through reading or other activities, to complete assigned work and process and apply the information learned on higher than a remembering level because the students do not understand the vocabulary necessary to be successful in their academic classes.

What strategies are teachers using to help students learn academic vocabulary and use the vocabulary in class?

#2: Students are expected to use academic vocabulary in every aspect of literacy during a class. Several trainings throughout the year have been done on ways to encourage students to comfortably use academic vocabulary when speaking, reading, and writing.

Are students correctly using academic vocabulary in all aspects of literacy during their class? *(reading, writing, listening, and speaking)*

Theory of action 2

If we require students to use correct English and academic vocabulary in all four aspects of literacy (reading, writing, listening, and speaking) during every class, then the students ability to learn, understand, and apply knowledge gained in every class will increase.

Linked problems of practice:

#1: Writing needs to be a part of every class. What writing activities are students doing in class? Are students using proper English and academic vocabulary during their writing assignments? (Not are the teachers telling students to use proper English and academic vocabulary, but are students actually using proper English and academic vocabulary in their writing activities.)

Source: Adapted with permission from Virginia Lannen, CEO, Pegasus School of Liberal Arts and Sciences, Dallas, Texas.

come in for, it's probably not taking place. The other issue is that we always come in on Tuesdays, and so there's a debate about whether teachers put the best lessons on Tuesday. I tell them that if this is the best lesson and we still see from the patterns and predictions that it needs to improve, then that tells us something important about what we need to teach. And if it's a great lesson, then at least we know that students are getting that once a week, then you know that they will be having an amazing lesson."

See exhibit 3.3 for a sample rounds observation schedule. Notice how the schedule for the visit day references the theory of action, literacy goals for the year, and the problem of practice.

After the Visit

The primary and very explicit follow-up from any rounds visit is the way that it shapes the subsequent cycle for the Wednesday professional development sessions. Cadre leaders return to the original problem of practice and, based on their readings and professional experience, organize and then deliver the next weeks of professional development. What happens after that varies by teacher. Hart describes it as a "mixed bag—some teachers are comfortable making the changes and feel like they've learned a lot." For the others, "We go through the cycle again, and we try different types of professional development, and maybe if they are a new teacher and they're just getting a handle on what's going on in the classroom and if we do it again, then maybe it will have a different kind of impact." The second kind of follow-up is a tight connection that Pegasus makes to the supervision and evaluation process. Although the school keeps a distinction between how data from observations and from rounds visits are used, it acknowledges that the "look-fors" may be the same or similar for both. In fact, Pegasus has recently restructured its formal observations to better align with its rounds processes. Hart observes, "So what we are looking for in rounds is what they are also trying to look for in the formal observations. So, for instance, we'll focus on literacy in the rounds, and on their formal evaluations, what literacy activities the students are doing. So even if some of the teachers are picking it up from rounds and others aren't, it will be addressed again in the formal observations." Because of that close alignment, and because some of the same people are doing formal observations as are doing instructional rounds, Pegasus tries to make it clear when people are being observed for formal observations—telling them in advance for the first time and then making clear that when someone comes in alone it's a formal observation, since the rounds visits are always done in pairs.

EXHIBIT 3.3

Sample rounds observation schedule

Theory of action:

If we require students to use correct English and academic vocabulary in all four aspects of literacy (reading, writing, listening, and speaking) during every class, then the students' ability to learn, understand, and apply knowledge gained in every class will increase.

Excerpt from Pegasus Literacy Goals of the Year:

• When was the last time your students had sore hands from writing in your class? Just like conversation, writing helps us make sense of what we are learning and helps us make connections to our own lives or others' ideas.

• You can't avoid thinking when you write.

• Students need to be writing every day, in every classroom. How about adding to your instruction more informal and fun writing activities like quick writes, stop and jots, one-minute essays, graffiti conversations? Not all writing assignments need to be formal ones.

Problem of practice:

Writing needs to be a part of every class. What writing activities are students doing in class? Are students using proper English and academic vocabulary during their writing assignments? (Not, are the teachers *telling* students to use proper English and academic vocabulary, but are students *actually using* proper English and academic vocabulary in their writing activities.)

Observations teams and schedules:

Meredith and Mike:	11:00–11:30	Room 237, 10th grade
	11:30–12:00	8/9 Cadre Mavs Orange, Art Room 226
	12:00–12:30	Room 263, 11th grade
Brandi and Clements:	11:00–11:30	Room 102-6/7 Cadre 1-Lion Cadre-Math
	11:30–12:00	6/7 Cadre 4 Hawkeye, Science Room 114
	12:00–12:30	K/1 Cadre Bears, Room 101
Christian and Casey:	11:00–11:30	Art/History 4/5 Cadre 2 Horned Frogs, Room 210
	11:30–12:00	2/3 Cadre, Room 104
	12:00–12:30	6/7 Cadre 2 Griffins, Writing Room 224

Source: Adapted with permission from Virginia Lannen, CEO, Pegasus School of Liberal Arts and Sciences, Dallas, Texas.

Hart notes that sorting out the difference between rounds and supervisory evaluations is a bigger issue in a school-based rounds setting, as opposed to a cross-school one: "Rounds is designed to enhance professional development and not evaluate a particular teacher. But because we do rounds so frequently, the teachers are used to having people coming in and watching, so they are much more comfortable with it than they would be if they were only observed once a year. Since you're observed every Tuesday as well as these formal observations, and since many classrooms are shared, there are people in and out of classrooms and being observed quite often."

CONNECTIONS TO SCHOOL IMPROVEMENT PRACTICES

Pegasus's CEO, Virginia Lannen, sees a strong connection between rounds and improvement:

> In years past, one of the things we struggled with is how to make connections between all the different work that we were doing. In the past it felt like we are doing rounds over here, and then this other professional development work was over there, and benchmarking stood alongside. This year, we really tried to make connections, and rounds is now the hub of the wheel and the spokes go out from it. Because we have implemented the cadre system, where cadre leaders meet weekly with their assigned cadres, cadre leaders (who are also our rounds team) have another opportunity to make connections. They can look at individuals and look at their lesson plans and say, "We are seeing what we are training on or maybe not," so that's another area where the teachers can get assistance. It really all ties together in ways that are much more connected than has been the past, so it is really quite tight.

To make this happen—to make it "tight"—Pegasus is using a theory of action that looks something like this: *If we identify areas that we can work on during the summer, if we can set up rounds with a focused professional development cycle immediately following, if we can involve all staff in the process, then we are going to focus on ways to improve instruction and therefore improve learning for our students.*

The strategic success of this theory of action hinges in large measure on the roles played by the cadre leaders. These individuals also represent a large investment of resources for the school—it is expensive to schedule five teachers to have one full day a week to observe, make sense of what they're observing, and plan professional development for the others. While the primary mechanism for transferring what this small group has learned to the rest of the faculty is through Wednesday professional development sessions, the leadership of the school has given some thought to some other modalities of involving the rest of the faculty. When Pegasus administrators and cadre leaders came to Harvard for the Rounds 2 Institute, they realized that the six veteran teachers involved in rounds didn't do that much sharing with the rest of the staff, so they developed approaches to try to make things much clearer to the staff. They trained the entire faculty to understand what rounds is to help them distinguish between rounds and formal observations. This is particularly important because Pegasus is a small school and some roles overlap, so an individual might be on a rounds visit one day and on an evaluation visit another. The school made a quick shorthand: "If we come in on a Tuesday and with a partner, then it is not evaluative." In addition, once every six or seven weeks, on a Wednesday, the rounds team brings to the entire staff one of the problems that it has already identified and discussed and all work together using the 5 Whys root cause analysis protocol. This allows the rounds team to get the perspective of the teachers (as well as a way for the teachers to understand and own the process better.) When they have done this, rounds teams sometimes find that the full staff may actually identify other root causes of the underlying problem, which enables them to plan staff development better, by using the insights of the full staff as well as their own.

A critical part of improving instruction is building the capacity of the teachers. This is particularly important at Pegasus with its relatively high turnover, especially among its new teachers. To do this, the school has been offering Wednesday professional development for years, but the teacher training was not nearly as tightly tied to rounds and classroom observations. Hart describes the changes in those Wednesday trainings:

> Now they are more focused on what takes place in the classroom, especially the work the students are doing. The first year we did rounds, we were focusing on the process and didn't spend as much time focusing on what students were doing. We got better at that after our first Institute at Harvard, but it still didn't really tie into what we did on Wednesdays. The goal is to focus on the task that the students are doing, and the rounds team is getting better at picturing how what we do during Wednesday professional development directly affects what goes on our classroom.

ASSESSING IMPACTS AND EVOLVING THE ROUNDS PRACTICE

To help track its improvement progress as a school, in addition to the rounds observations, Pegasus uses repeated assessments of individual students. Every few months, students take a benchmark in classes that are tested on the state test, which the school uses to see which areas of study the students still need help on. They also use some online programs that track individual student accomplishment on the required standards for learning, including one that lets students log in and monitor their own progress. But mostly it relies on observations in rounds to track progress: "The most systematic part," says Virginia Hart, "is what we see in classroom practices when we go in for rounds, secondly through formal observations, and then more anecdotally what we notice about teachers helping each other out or leadership helping them."

To illustrate the type of improvement loops that are central to Pegasus's strategy, Hart tells the full version of the story that was referred to in the opening vignette:

This year we started focusing on using academic vocabulary. Since we have lots of English as a second language learners, we've seen that it ends up being easier for students and for teachers not to use academic vocabulary. For instance, in math classes, instead of referring to the numerator and denominator, teachers and students will often refer to the "top "and the "bottom" of the fraction. So we decided to use that as the problem of practice for our October rounds cycle. The rounds team—five cadre leaders whose teaching schedules are kept free on Tuesdays, and the school director—started the three-week cycle with classroom visits and debriefing, complete with observations, patterns, and predictions.

Not surprisingly, in the first week's cycle, they noticed only a few teachers were really trying to use academic vocabulary or to ask the students to do it. The following Tuesday, when they met, they tried to figure out what some of the underlying reasons for that were. They used the 5 Whys protocol that they had learned at Harvard [Graduate School of Education] and focused on the fact that most of our teachers were new and were simply not comfortable with the academic vocabulary. Based on that, when they met the following Tuesday, the rounds team planned what the next cycle of staff development for teachers should be. First, the rounds team brought in some worksheets that would provide easy ways to weave language into the classroom. They also arranged to have an outside specialist on academic language come in to speak to the group, and organized a book study of *Making Learning Visible* so that teachers could find ways to connect with the kids to understand academic vocabulary.[1]

We did this in October, and then in early December cycled back with the same focus to see what kind of improvement had taken place. I was excited about that, because we wanted to show that the cycle could actually lead to improvement. The rounds team was pleasantly surprised with the results that we observed. The team discovered that there has been an increase in the number of teachers that actively use and model academic vocabu-lary (the listening and speaking aspects of literacy). There was also an increase, albeit smaller, in the number of students who are also using vocabulary when discussing academic topics with each other and with the teacher.

While the rounds team did not observe an increase in use of academic vocabulary in other areas of literacy (e.g., writing and reading), all of us were excited to observe its use by teachers and students when speaking with and listening to each other. As a result, the rounds team can now appreciate the repetitiveness of the problem of practice when observing classes, because they can see positive results and growth from the process we have developed. Moreover, they have a direction for next steps with respect to professional development.

Hart hopes that revisiting the same problem of practice a few cycles later will give teachers an appreciation of what the improvement cycle can look like, to make tangible connections between the observation, the professional development cycle, and the subsequent changes in practice that show up in classrooms. She has been very pleased to see exactly those kinds of data in the academic vocabulary story, knowing that that will contribute to a common sense of collective efficacy, and help boost the commitment of the teachers and of the school administration to the rounds process.

Virginia Lannen concludes: "It was eye-opening for me at the Rounds 2 Institute to realize that it's really all about how rounds can lift the whole organization—lift the whole boat. Even though I had read that in the first book [*Instructional Rounds in Education*] and I know that in rounds you are not critiquing individual teach-ers, I realize now that rounds is really for the benefit of the organization and the students we serve . . . It is really not about utilizing it for individuals. For me when I try to visualize this, I think it would be good to have something like a fundrais-ing thermometer to show them at the Wednesday training—to see how rounds is moving the work of the whole school forward."

CHAPTER 4

School-Based Rounds in a Midsize Urban District
Akron Public Schools

Rick Sims was pleasantly surprised with the discussion that followed the feedback he and his fellow science teachers were getting. The seven members of Garfield High School's math department had spent two hours observing in science classrooms and the rest of the day comparing observation notes, naming patterns and predictions, and formulating next-level-of-work suggestions. It was about twenty minutes into the final portion of the visit day—when the math teachers gave feedback to the science teachers and then discussed with them the implications of the visit for each department—that Rick Sims started to smile.

The day before, when the math teachers had been briefed about the science department's problem of practice, they had listened politely when Rick and his colleagues asked them to pay particular attention to the student responses to higher-level questions and indicated that the science teachers felt stuck about getting good, higher-level responses. The math teachers said they would certainly look for data on this issue, but they were quite sure that wasn't an area of trouble for them.

Rick thought at the time how typical that was for teachers. "They are so reluctant to observe out of the disciplines," he had thought to himself. "Teachers want to observe each other—math wants to observe math, science wants to observe science, because they think that their practices are so different from each other." Rick, who was not only a science teacher at Garfield but a rounds facilitator for the district, had a different opinion—that, in fact, many of the patterns in classrooms were similar across all departments.

So it was around 2:15, after the math teachers came to share with the science professional learning community what they had observed and what they thought of it, that Rick saw the "aha" moment as they made the connection to their own teaching. That morning, they had seen consistent patterns of "rescuing" kids. They had noticed how science teachers would often pose rich questions and then, before kids really had an opportunity to answer them, the teachers would answer them themselves or add so much structure the kids didn't do any work. During the robust conversation that took place after these patterns were shared, it turned out the math teachers had thought they were running into trouble in a different area, but after observing, they realized that what they saw in the science classes was actually more of an issue for them as well.

Rick was pleased to see this. It reminded him of some things that he had come to notice about rounds. "When it is all said and done," he thought, "no matter where the sticking point is, a lot of the patterns are very similar across all the departments. Even though we approach it from a different point of view, the patterns came out all the same. It actually kind of unifies us. To see that were all working on the same kind of work and were all having the same kind of issues. And it's always the case that the observing teachers get a lot out of the day."

As he packed up for the day, Rick was satisfied that both the observed department and the visiting department had gotten something meaningful from the day. He started thinking about some readings that he might share about "rescuing"—not just with his colleagues in the science department, but with those in the math department as well.

BACKGROUND AND CONTEXT

Even before they heard about instructional rounds, Akron Public Schools had articulated an overarching goal: "Create a culture of examining our professional practice." From the minute the district started to learn the rounds practice in 2007 as part of the Ohio Leadership Collaborative—working with the Harvard rounds team and four other districts—it saw rounds as a means to creating that culture. By the end of the first year, all the participating districts had to prepare and then launch a local plan for in-district, cross-school rounds. Akron did so, but saw cross-school practice (what it calls *external rounds*) as a way to develop a practice for what it really wanted—school-based (or *internal*) rounds.

Akron actualized this plan by setting up networks of five schools that would conduct cross-school rounds for two (or in some cases, three) years, to develop a practice, build capacity, and help train and identify teachers who could then facilitate internal rounds. During their last year in the cross-school network, the schools each prepared and shared their local plans for internal rounds, to be launched the following school year. The plans had to include several nonnegotiable elements of

---

Instructional Rounds in Akron Public Schools

- Urban district of fifty schools, half of which are doing school-based rounds
- Engaged in instructional rounds since 2007
- Districtwide rounds as launching pad for school-based instructional rounds: schools "graduate" from cross-school rounds to internal rounds after two to three years
- Local variation encouraged; network composition varies:
  - Garfield High School pairs departments to observe and debrief
  - Crouse Community Learning Center asks grade-level teams to invite observation
- Semiannual cycle
- Anchored in schoolwide problems of practice
- Linked to improvement through districtwide rubric

---

rounds—a problem of practice, nonjudgmental observational notes, some form of patterning and suggestions—but each school otherwise had flexibility to create an internal rounds structure that met its unique developmental needs. Consequently, Akron has an array of school-based rounds models in place. The district sees the variations of internal rounds practice as key to building a broader district culture of having educators "examining professional practice." The case study describes the common elements for internal rounds practice in Akron, as well as the variations that take place at two schools.

THE PRACTICE
Before the Visit

Three elements must be in place for a rounds visit—a problem of practice, a prepared faculty who understand what a rounds visit is, why it is done, and how to participate in one, and one or more facilitators to guide the practice.

Across all Akron public schools, the problem of practice is developed with the entire staff in a process facilitated by the School Improvement Plan team. Staff are trained by and supported by Akron rounds facilitators. All schools are expected to have a locally developed problem of practice that is connected to other school improvement efforts; this becomes the basis for any instructional rounds visits. However, local teams within a school—for instance, departments at the secondary schools—have the option of picking a more focused problem of practice for their internal rounds visits that fits under and is related to the school problem of practice.

To prepare a staff when a school is first launching internal rounds, a two-hour training session is offered to members who are unfamiliar with the rounds process. This is important, since, unless they are among the few who have served on one of the external rounds visit teams, prior to starting internal rounds, many teachers' only exposure to rounds may have been being visited. These teachers get to practice by observing a video of classroom instruction, providing nonjudgmental comments, and patterning those comments. For Sharon Hall, one of Akron's facilitator trainers, the biggest benefit is that teachers realize that the process is truly not designed to be judging of them as individuals. Hall notes that as part of this training and orientation, teachers often will do some additional readings about rounds. Overall, she finds these orientation sessions helpful in giving teachers a good idea of what rounds is and what it is not.

Akron provides districtwide training for the facilitators who will prepare for, conduct, and follow up school-based rounds visits. Early rounds adopters like Hall, who is coordinator of gifted and talented services, and Rick Sims, a high school science teacher, are both facilitators who support the work of the in-school facilitators for school-based rounds. In fact, one of the core ideas in Akron's model has been that teachers or instructional coaches serve as facilitators, with minimal facilitation from administrators. Ellen McWilliams, the assistant superintendent who has overseen the development of rounds as part of Akron's strategic improvement, explains this commitment: "We firmly believe that this [rounds] practice is about teachers examining their own practice and learning from other practitioners like them. It absolutely is also about principals and curriculum staff learning a common language and gaining consensus around high-quality teaching and learning. The foundation of this work, though, has to be about teachers working collaboratively and opening up their practice with each other. The only way in my perspective to really facilitate a classroom-based discussion and to keep it in that place is to have teacher leaders facilitating it."

Akron created a recruitment and facilitation development pipeline that worked in tandem with its two-year process of using external rounds as the training ground for school-based or internal rounds. Each school team participating in external rounds included the principal and four teachers. By the end of year one of the cross-school rounds, trainers and district facilitators had identified potential school-based facilitators in each school and provided additional support and training for them in year two. Support including monthly meetings, readings, practice in asking probing questions, skills in how to help build capacity, how to "read " a roomful of adult learners, when to interject, and when to wait. During year two, the system facilitators would transfer as much responsibility to the school-based teachers as possible, encouraging them to plan and facilitate as much of the rounds visit at their own school as they were comfortable.

At the Visit

Beyond this common preparation, the actual visits, visit structures, and follow-up processes vary considerably. All schools can use a certain amount of substitute money for conducting internal rounds, based on enrollments, percentage of students eligible for free and reduced-price lunches, and school improvement status as determined by the School Improvement (Title 1) Office. Schools have the option of getting full- or half-day substitutes or of using the money to pay teachers for planning or debriefing time after school. Two examples of local variation are described below.

Garfield High School.   At Garfield High School, where twelve hundred students are grouped into one of three career pathways in a massive brick building dating from the 1920s, departments are paired, so that science and math teachers will visit one another, as will social studies and language arts teachers. The day before the visit, in its professional learning community time, the department that will be visited the next day will explain the stuck point that its members have identified within the school's broader problem of practice and outline what they would like their colleagues to pay particular attention to. On the visit day, in two teams of three or four, the observing teachers will visit four classrooms, observing the first and second half of two periods (see exhibit 4.1). The observers will then move through the usual stages of the rounds protocol, by sharing descriptive data, patterns, predictions and next-level-of-work suggestions (sometimes framing these with reflective questions, an approach that some of the Ohio districts use for the next-level-of-work portion of the practice). At the end of this process, in contrast to cross-school rounds, the observers will present their observations and suggestions directly to the department that has been visited and discuss with them the implications of the observations for both departments. These reciprocal visits are designed to take place twice a year (see exhibit 4.2).

Crouse Community Learning Center.   At Crouse Community Learning Center, a recently renovated elementary school serving 450 students, teachers choose to make the visits more individualized and personal. Although there is an annual

---

EXHIBIT 4.1

Garfield HS schedule

Science department internal rounds visitation schedule

Math team A	Math team B
Sax	Seiler
Sibbio	Ibraham
Reno	Gregory
Vukotic	Morgan
Paradise	Kalain
	Sims

Team	Time	Subject	Room number
A	9:10–9:30	Biology	118
B	9:10–9:30	Physical science	305
B	9:35–9:55	Biology	118
A	9:35–9:55	Physical science	305
A	10:05–10:25	Chemistry	302
B	10:05–10:25	Physics	301
B	10:30–10:50	Chemistry	302
A	10:30–10:50	Physics	301
Return to the president's room at 11:00 a.m.			

Source: Adapted with permission from Ellen McWilliams, Assistant Superintendent, Curriculum and Instruction, Akron Public Schools, Ohio.

EXHIBIT 4.2

Garfield High School rounds agenda

Science department internal rounds agenda

Day before the visit

1:42–2:30	President's room	• Meet with science professional learning communities (both physical and life science). • Establish stuck points around problem of practice. • Formulate focus questions for tomorrow's visit. • Share visitation schedule and remind them of wrap-up/share-out session.

Day of visit

8:00–8:10	President's room	Welcome, agenda, review norms
8:10–8:50		Bloom's sorting activity
8:50–9:00		Review of focus questions and classroom visit protocols
9:00–11:00	Classrooms	Classroom visits
11:00–12:00	President's room	Debrief begins: Affinity protocol (sort), patterns established, begin predictions
12:00–12:30	On your own	Lunch
12:35–1:15	President's room	Finish predictions/share-out
1:15–1:40		Next level of work/ share-out/consensus on next level of work
1:42–2:30		Joint share out of visit with Math and Science departments

After the visit (within one week of visit)

1:42–2:30	PLC room	Debrief visit with Science professional learning communities, plot next steps for next level of work
2:30–3:24		Debrief visit with Math professional learning community, establish from visit connections to work of Math Department

Source: Adapted with permission from Ellen McWilliams, Assistant Superintendent, Curriculum and Instruction, Akron Public Schools, Ohio.

schoolwide problem of practice, each grade-level team gets to request specific feedback from the observation team. For principal Angela Harper-Brooks, inviting this level of customization and personalization is key to gaining teacher ownership and investment in the process. In her view, "When you come in and observe me, I'm going to listen more to what you say and I am more likely to make a change if I had a chance to influence what you're focusing on." For example, underneath the umbrella of a schoolwide problem of practice focusing on student engagement and the use of accountable talk in the classroom, a teaching team might request specific feedback on what happens to the groups of students working independently (what are they doing and talking about) while the teacher is teaching a small-group lesson. This customized focus is outlined at the start of the visit day and the data collected on it are left along with all the other data at the end of the visit. Unlike at Garfield, the observers do not stay to discuss the feedback with the host teachers. (There is a teacher leader who participates on the visit and is available for such discussions.) With a staff of three teachers on each grade as well as three special education teachers, Crouse has experimented with having the third-, fourth-, and fifth-grade teachers collectively visit the primary grades and then vice versa. Another year, the school mixed the teachers into vertical teams, divided them in half, and then had each group visit one another. Visits are done twice a year.

After the Visit

Just as the development of a problem of practice (and its connection to the school's improvement plan) before a visit is, at least in theory, common and consistent across all of Akron's schools, so too is the expectation that a rounds visit will lead to results that will be connected back into the school's improvement processes, usually through the professional learning communities.

At Garfield, the whole internal visit cycle is structured around the professional learning community. At the front end, a particular department uses its professional learning community structure to identify the focus for its problem of practice. On the day of the visit, when the observers are giving direct feedback, it is to the host department's professional learning community, and the follow-up is housed in and managed through the department's professional learning community. For example, the opening vignette for this chapter described a recent visit to the science department at Garfield High, which provided insights about higher-order thinking questions and about how teachers were "rescuing" students (see exhibit 4.3).

EXHIBIT 4.3

Garfield High School science rounds results summary

Garfield High School Science Department internal rounds

The following represents the results from the instructional rounds visit of our science classrooms conducted by the Math Department. As discussed in the rounds wrap-up meeting held with the Math Department, we should be cognizant of the patterns and next-level-of-work suggestions as we plan future instruction. These results will also help to drive our PLC meetings in the future.

Focus questions:

Although we have made an effort to incorporate higher-level thinking opportunities into our daily instruction, we have asked the Math Department to be cognizant of the following areas during their visit:

- Types/levels (according to Bloom's taxonomy) of questions asked to students
- Levels of responses to questions formulated by students
- Levels of thinking required during instructional time
- Motivational quality of questions/assignments

Patterns:

- Majority of questions were low-level, rapid-fire questions
- Majority of student responses were low-level
- Higher-level questions were most often answered by the teacher ("rescuing")
- Some use of short formative assessments to check understanding were evident, but the results were often ignored (teachers continued forward with instruction despite evidence of students not understanding)

Next level of work:

- How can you as a department purposefully raise the levels of questioning on a daily/weekly basis?
- What strategies could be utilized to avoid rescuing students before they answer higher-level questions?
- How can you create an environment that allows *all* students to demonstrate understanding other than a test and what do you do when they don't understand?

Source: Adapted with permission from Ellen McWilliams, Assistant Superintendent, Curriculum and Instruction, Akron Public Schools, Ohio.

Rick Sims describes what the science professional learning community did after the visit: "The pattern was that we were giving some opportunities for students for higher order thinking skills but it would fall flat because of rescuing. So we knew that as a science department, we needed to challenge kids with rich projects." The professional learning community decided to work collaboratively to have the students do science-fair projects. To prevent the continuation of their pattern—giving out high-level assignments but accepting low-level student work—the science teachers decided that they would keep bringing the work back to the team at each stage. Sims notes that this was a marked departure from past practice: "This was unusual for us because none of us did much in common except cover the content in the same way. Or, really, we would cover the same content in a number different ways, so it was very unusual for us to work together." At each stage of the process, teachers checked in with their peers to make sure they weren't repeating their old pattern. They brought student project proposals back to the professional learning community and agreed together what would be acceptable and what would not. With common calibrated understandings of what was acceptable, they were able to push the students further. Sims concludes, "Now these common projects are spurring us in other ways where we were really kind of falling flat—and we've even gotten to the point where we are starting to develop common lessons, common assessments and it's really brought along the professional learning community process."

At Crouse, professional learning communities are also central to the follow-up. It is while working in them that teachers get access to the feedback notes from the visitors, and it is in those same groups that teachers work on the consequent improvement. The professional learning communities in Crouse are also at the heart of another strong connection that Crouse makes between rounds and instructional improvement. For three weeks each year, each community has had several half days of substitute release time and an external coach to help its members work together to polish and implement specific lessons designed to address some of their stuck points in the school's problem of practice. It is during this cycle that the instructional rounds are conducted; and the data from those rounds are used as an important input in their improvement cycle. In fact, principal Harper-Brooks sees a close and symbiotic connection between rounds and the professional learning community improvement cycle. "The only way that we're going to get better is if we see what other people are doing and we give each other feedback on it. Instructional rounds has opened the door that lets us go in and get personal in looking at each other's practice . . . Then later, when people see that they need to improve on something, they know that they can turn to their colleagues for ideas and for help."

In general, follow-up procedures and expectations, including what accountability structures are put into place to support them, vary widely from school to school. Since the system has deliberately given schools the autonomy to develop their own customized instructional rounds models, the practices across the schools are different. Consequently, follow-up processes are not consistently built into the rounds process. "It is less formal," says assistant superintendent Ellen McWilliams, "because you don't have a lot of checks and balances built in. You lose some of the formality of the [rounds] event." She makes clear that she expects evidence-based discussions from the rounds visits to feed into the improvement work at the schools, particularly through the professional learning communities, but notes that she has varied levels of confidence in exactly what happens by way of follow-up in each of the schools: "There isn't any external commitment that gets reported out; it is all about what goes on in the internal commitments at the school."

Akron has instead turned to school improvement teams to help monitor use of rounds data as part of the instructional improvement cycle at the school level. In addition, McWilliams expects teams to use their professional learning community structure to move from "Now, here we have some new data that we saw today" to discussion of what adjustments in classrooms need to happen. Ideally the professional learning community will also build in monitoring processes to not only commit to the adjustments but to following them up with subsequent observations. But McWilliams acknowledges that this is still quite variable: "You can't separate rounds from the school improvement process. If you have high-quality professional learning communities then part of the protocol that we train teams on is that when you have that discussion [after a rounds visit], you write into the minutes: here is what we looked at, here is what we committed to over the next month, here's when we will to come back to the table to discuss it, here is the data that we will use to see if the adjustments actually worked. So it is built into the process."

CONNECTIONS TO SCHOOL AND DISTRICT IMPROVEMENT PRACTICES

With a rounds practice that has been deliberately decentralized and focused on creating a culture where staff would regularly "examine its professional practice," Akron Public Schools has had to be very strategic about ensuring that rounds would ultimately lead to school improvement. By investing so much in development of rounds and shifting so much of the focus for improvement to the individual schools, Akron has learned how critical individual school capacity is in creating a link between rounds and improvement.

After noticing that some schools "got" rounds and were making the hoped-for culture changes but others did not, Akron found it helpful when, last year, members of the Harvard Graduate School of Education rounds team shared a school rubric that identified different domains of school capacity (leadership, teaming, use of data, etc.) "It was like the heavens opened up," McWilliams said about seeing it, "and it made sense for us that the rounds work is really just a way to have this culture created—of examining our professional practice. Once we are able to integrate rounds with the full picture of school improvement across all those aspects, then it really made sense to us in terms of how to approach buildings. We can see that the buildings that have continued to use the internal rounds and fit them into their school improvement strategies, can do this because they have at least part of these aspects [from the rubric] of school improvement in place."

Inspired by this insight into the importance of school capacity building, Akron developed a theory of action that put capacity-building front and center as part of it approach to improvement (see exhibit 4.4). The district created its own version of rubric that looked at where each school was on six domains: their use of *data*, the collective efficacy and self-directedness of their *collaborative planning teams*, the ownership and learning focus of their *problems of practice*, the strength of the research base of their instructional *strategies*, the clarity of the processes put into place to implement and monitor the way teachers go about *adjusting instruction*, the existence of shared *building leadership (teachers and administrators)* that is clearly focused on instruction; and the tight alignment of all the school's initiatives with one another and the improvement strategy in a strong *connectivity of school improvement initiatives*. The appendix at the end of this chapter shows the rubric in full.

Once the rubric was in place, the district could be much more strategic about improvement. McWilliams gives the example of how a school that was deficient in some in those areas would come to rounds over and over again, and get angrier and angrier because there was nothing to connect it to: "It made zero sense to them because they didn't have the professional learning communities in place and they didn't have a leader who understood it or could help them connect the dots." If, on their developmental rubric, school staff identified that everything needed to improve, then the key for McWilliams was to actually support them in developing

---

EXHIBIT 4.4

Theory of action for school improvement in Akron Public Schools

If we create a culture of examining our professional practice, and . . .

> If all staff are engaged in or supporting high-quality teaching and learning;

> If the district develops and builds capacity for a framework for instruction that impacts the instructional core and uses that framework to guide and direct the practice of all staff to build a common understanding of high-quality teaching and learning characteristics;

> If teams of staff members are engaged in examining their practice through facilitated SIP processes, professional learning communities, instructional rounds, and other embedded ongoing professional development;

> If leaders at all levels (teacher leaders, principals, central office) create a safe and trusting environment in order for all staff to examine and improve their practice;

> If staff have a voice in decision making and in building internal accountability for teaching and learning;

. . . *then* staff will be knowledgeable, instruction will be rigorous, students will be engaged, and we will dramatically increase student attainment.

Source: Adapted with permission from Ellen McWilliams, Assistant Superintendent, Curriculum and Instruction, Akron Public Schools, Ohio.

the capacity to improve and to use rounds as part of that improvement, but not expect that rounds alone could do it. She noted, "We could provide a menu of supports if they identify that they don't understand how to use data, or their leadership doesn't really know how to move forward, or they struggle with how to properly develop a problem of practice." She acknowledges that it is hard to do this for fifty schools, but says there is no other work that is more important for the central office: "We can provide the specific approaches that are tailored to that building."

For the district, this was a strategic insight: if central office does not calibrate, monitor, and support these domains of capacity at the school level, there is no point in investing in rounds and the district cannot expect school improvement. McWilliams adds:

> There are inputs and barriers that impact the success of their ability to improve their practice . . . We believe that it doesn't make it impossible, but it does make it more difficult to have the dialogue around high-quality teaching and learning and to have it nurtured, because there's no time in your day to talk about it. You can have a rounds visit, and . . . if you got this incredible data, but if you don't have your professional learning communities operating in a way that allows it to naturally be discussed, it makes it much more difficult. Obviously, teacher leadership and principal leadership is a huge piece. One of the things that our rubric addresses is connectivity—if you don't have coherence about what you're currently doing and how it all connects, then you could be bringing in great evidence on this reading strategy, and you don't even get why you're doing this reading strategy . . . It does not make it impossible but it does make it much harder.

For how this effort fits into the overall improvement cycle for Akron Public Schools, see exhibit 4.5.

ASSESSING IMPACTS AND EVOLVING THE ROUNDS PRACTICE

To track the progress of the school-level instructional improvement, in addition to the use of test scores and state ratings, Akron Public Schools uses two kinds of data sources to track school improvement capacity on its developmental rubric. One is self-assessment done by each school (after training and calibration on the instrument). The second is by a "PACE" team, a group of administrators who, using the same rubric, makes an assessment annually at each school. Along with this monitoring come strong and specifically targeted forms of support—three doses of professional development– or professional learning community–based embedded

EXHIBIT 4.5

Akron Public Schools instructional improvement cycle

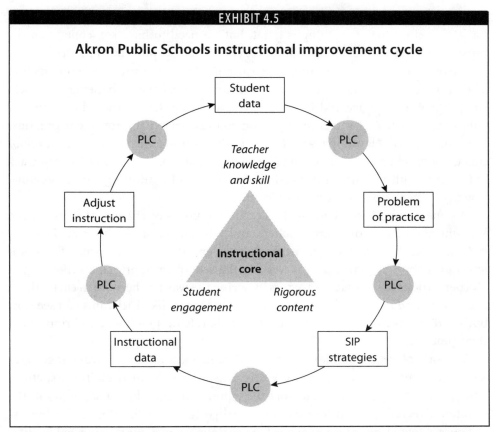

Source: Adapted with permission from Ellen McWilliams, Assistant Superintendent, Curriculum and Instruction, Akron Public Schools, Ohio.

support a year; for instance, on what it means to work in a quality professional learning community. This is the nature of the strategic commitment that Akron has made to this school-by-school approach to improvement.

In addition, the district, which has been using external (cross-school) rounds primarily as a way to scale up and launch internal (school-based) rounds, is considering ways to use them as an additional data source. Ellen McWilliams notes the need for continued external calibration: "When we have gotten to full internal rounds, we will still be supporting external rounds—at least once a year, although a school could ask for more. Angela [Harper-Brooks, principal at Crouse] put it well when she said, 'We could be hanging out internally patting ourselves on the back, thinking that everything is great, but we need to have someone from the outside come in to offer some calibration and to help us push our practice.'"

Akron's strategy of welcoming wide variation in rounds practice across its fifty schools encourages innovation and, at the same time, creates challenges in tracking progress on the use and impacts of the rounds practice. The school capacity rubric helps, with its integration of non-rounds-related improvement practices like collaborative planning teams with rounds-specific processes like the development of a problem of practice. The Akron leadership team also tries to keep track of the larger culture shift—the creation of a "culture of examining our professional practice." There are no easy metrics for this.

On one hand, McWilliams is thrilled by the kinds of changes that have been brought about. Not only are teachers and administrators looking at data and reflecting on the practice, but she notes with enthusiasm that teams of custodians and school secretaries are as well. At the school level, principals like Angela Harper-Brooks can measure progress by seeing the way teachers are in each other's classrooms and learning from one another, or teachers like Rick Sims can see slow but steady steps as high school teachers collaborate on looking at and improving their practice.

At another level, McWilliams and her colleagues know that culture change takes a long time and is taking place very unevenly across the district. The structural and system changes need to support the culture changes, but at some point, the collaborative, reflective culture should—ideally—take over. She notes: "The big lesson here is that we now know we need to continue support for the internal facilitators to ensure we're staying true to the nonnegotiables. We're currently scheduling a meeting for early February of all of the 'graduates of the cross-district rounds' to review the internal rounds action plans they developed and set up a more formal structure for them to access the funds for subs, extended time, etc. . . . It's all about the systems you put in place to support the process as you move from external to internal." At the same time, McWilliams is deliberately hoping for a phasing out of formal structures after two years or so of internal rounds—that practice will be open and the culture of reflecting on and refining professional practice will be sufficiently rooted to eventually make the mandated structures unnecessary. But she wonders how to account for the different developmental trajectories in the different schools and how much to try to keep protocols and other accountability structures related to rounds in place: "It's a trade-off. If we are trying to create a culture where this is happening naturally, do we have to be real careful with the protocols, do we have to keep training, do we have to keep revisiting and bringing facilitators in to reinforce that? I am not sure of that answer. It may not be that important once you build it into the culture."

McWilliams does know, and speaks with considerable certitude, about the impact that rounds has had and its close interconnection with instructional improvement in Akron: "Rounds shines a spotlight on the strengths and weaknesses that you have in your school improvement process as a whole." But it does not replace or become the school improvement process, she continues: "It is not about rounds. It is all about the culture that exists around improvement practices at the school. The whole internal rounds process is heavily, heavily contingent on these practices that exist within the culture of the school." McWilliams, who now devotes a significant portion of her central office staff to supporting the developmental capacity at the school sites, describes this as one of the most powerful lessons: "I wish we'd have learned it two years before."

Akron Public Schools developmental rubric for school improvement

Domain/Level	Beginning	Developing	Nearing proficient	Proficient
Data	• Any data gathered is used by individual teachers for the purpose of improvements in curriculum and instruction at the classroom level. • The primary focus of the classroom teacher is in preparing students to succeed in a variety of assessments.	• One basic source of data is relied on to improve curriculum and instruction. • Data review and revisions in curriculum and instruction occur on an annual basis. • Teachers understand that formative assessment practices are valuable for informing and enhancing instruction during the course of a lesson or unit.	• Improvement in curriculum and instruction occurs on an annual basis and is organized around school improvement committees. • More than one source of data is used when determining modifications in curriculum and instruction. • Some teachers are giving on-going formative assessments during the course of a lesson or unit.	• Improvement in curriculum and instruction is data-driven, on-going, systematic and collaborative. • Individual teachers and teacher teams continuously assess, adjust curricula and instruction, and assess again through the use of multiple sources of data until student targets are met. • All teachers periodically conduct formative assessments during the course of a lesson or unit to enhance instruction and to provide themselves and their students concrete information on how to improve individual student performance.

Domain/Level	Beginning	Developing	Nearing proficient	Proficient
Collaborative planning teams (CPTs)	• Teachers meet, but primarily work independently with a focus on teacher input and planning, not student learning outcomes • Beginning awareness of strategies, methods or materials other teachers use. • Some data is collected and used to inform and drive learning and teaching practices.	• Teams make basic decisions with some impact on instruction. • Teams periodically question and assess practice. • Some strategies and resources are implemented. • The collection and use of data to inform and develop teaching and learning is strong in some areas and weaker in others across the schools/CPTs.	• Teams have analyzed student achievement data and established goals to improve collaborative work with positive impact on instruction. • Teams use a variety of methods to investigate learning and teaching across the school/district with increasing consistency. • Teams work interdependently and learn by working together.	• CPTs are self-directed teams that strive for continuous improvement. • The CPT is a powerful form of professional development that is job-embedded and an integral part of the way the teachers work. • Teams question and assess current practice and seek areas of improvement. • Teams collect, analyze and use multiple sources of data to support decision making as evidenced by increased student achievement.
Problem of practice (POP)	• The problem of practice is driven by select data and does not resonate with the staff. • The problem of practice is developed to meet a compliance requirement for the SIP.	• Data is examined and more than one data source is used. • The problem of practice is predominately strategy-driven once the data identifies an initial issue of student performance.	• The problem of practice is developed based on root cause identified through multiple data sources/ • Strategies to address the problem of practice are implemented school-wide, but some inconsistencies exist.	• The problem of practice is embraced by staff and there is a clear causal link between the problem of practice and a clear learner problem uncovered by data. • Classroom practice is impacted by the problem of practice.

continued

Domain/Level	Beginning	Developing	Nearing proficient	Proficient
Strategies	• Instructional practices at the school emphasize the memorization of content and repeated practice of isolated skills. • Staff believe that all learners should be exposed to the same strategies regardless of learning style or cultural background.	• The instructional plans of some staff members are written to take into account the diverse needs of their students based on data. • Individual teachers are exploring best practice and are beginning to implement new strategies in the classroom.	• Some instructional plans have components built from insights on modern learning research, such as activities that activate prior student understanding, teaching of metacognition and/or those that provide opportunities for students to practice higher-level thinking using their mastery of standards-aligned content knowledge. • Technology is an important component in the differentiation of instructional practices.	• All instructional plans have components built from insights on modern learning research, such as activities that activate prior student understanding, teaching metacognition and/or providing opportunities for students to practice higher-level thinking. • Structured practices are in place for staff to research, implement, and evaluate best practice instructional strategies, including the effective use of technology. • Instructional practices are selected to align to the type of learning target (knowledge, reasoning, skill, performance or disposition) of the benchmark(s) and the matched assessment method(s) selected.

Domain/Level	Beginning	Developing	Nearing proficient	Proficient
Adjusting Instruction	• Current instructional practices are seen to be the best methods to deliver a large amount of content over time. Staff believe that its current modes of instructional practice are best suited to the student population that it serves.	• The delivered curriculum is designed for the average ability range of the student population. • Structures are in place to utilize the results of assessments to respond to individual student needs. This system relies primarily upon specialists within the school to provide the interventions for students. There is limited coordination between the specialist and classroom teacher.	• A system is in place that allows for teams of teachers to have a dialogue about instructional practices based on the schools' curriculum framework. • In order to improve student success in meeting the standards, some teachers employ a variety of instructional strategies geared to meet the varied needs of the student population. • Results of assessments are used to respond to individual student needs. Some general classroom teachers share in the responsibility to provide the interventions along with specialists.	• A formal process is in place to monitor curriculum delivery in the classroom and occurs in an on-going, scheduled manner. This process provides data that results in modifications to the school's delivered curriculum. • Teachers agree to employ a variety of common instructional strategies as appropriate in their lessons designed to meet the varied needs of the students. • A process is in place for teams to review individual student data to identify needs and design interventions. This data is shared with the student and parent on a regular basis and improvement goals are the outcome. • Teachers work closely with other support staff to monitor the student's progress. Students not demonstrating adequate progress are provided additional resources and opportunities to be successful. All staff share in providing interventions.

continued

APPENDIX: CHAPTER 4 *(continued)*

Domain/Level	Beginning	Developing	Nearing proficient	Proficient
Building leadership (teachers and administrators)	• Leadership has not conveyed a clear instructional focus. • Leadership intermittently observes and monitors instruction.	• Leadership is developing an instructional focus but there is a lack of shared understanding among teachers. • Observational practices are in place solely for compliance.	• Evidence of shared understanding of instructional focus. • Observational practices are in place that impact instruction. • Some evidence of Response to Intervention (RTI): high quality universal instruction, including acceleration, and targeted and intensive interventions.	• Instructional focus present in language and practice. • Building leadership routinely models their own knowledge of instructional practice with teachers. • Teachers share the vision and demonstrate commitment to making changes in their instructional practice. • Clear evidence of Response to Intervention (RTI): high quality universal instruction, including acceleration, and targeted and intensive interventions.
Connectivity of school improvement initiatives	• Several improvement efforts occurring but they do not support one another nor do they build on each other. • Little evidence to suggest that the efforts are making a meaningful impact.	• Some of the improvement efforts are linked in some way. • Little evidence of an overarching strategy that is focusing the work for the staff.	• An overarching strategy is in place and is embraced by most of the staff. • Not all of the school improvement work is focused under this strategy.	• A clear overarching strategy is in place and embraced by nearly all staff. • All the initiatives and school improvement work of the staff is aligned with this focused strategy.

Source: Adapted from work by Richard Elmore (Harvard Graduate School of Education) and the Michigan Department of Education (School Improvement Framework Rubrics).

CHAPTER 5

Connecting School-Based Rounds to District Improvement

Farmington Public Schools

The twelve students are ready. They are poised, self-confident, and very matter-of-fact, even though they know they will be making history this morning—the first students observing on a school-based rounds visit in Farmington. They gather in the high school library with an equal number of adults—guest observers and school and district administrators—drinking juice and eating muffins as the observation team is starting to assemble. One of the students is smiling as he points to out his friends the big sign posted: "No food or drink in the library. This means you!"

The previous week, these students had watched a classroom video to practice taking detailed nonjudgmental notes and to learn the rounds observation and debriefing cycle. They know the focus today will be on "purposeful engagement," one of the five key ideas in the district's instructional framework. A few of them had been a part of a process to advise administrators on what engagement might look like in classrooms. They have come prepared for this morning, which they know will be a partial rounds visit—observations, patterns, and prediction but no next level of work. Tom, a senior, has borrowed the *Instructional Rounds in Education* book to see what it is all about.[1] Charles is eager to get into classrooms and talk to students. "I'm a student too," he says, "They will be more honest with me, since I am one of them." Alice, a sophomore, is curious about seeing a variety of classes, including those for non-honors students.

After a short briefing by the assistant principal focusing on the "look-fors" around engagement, the students are mixed in with adults to form observation groups of four and five. They observe in three classrooms, looking at the tasks that had been assigned and the work that students were actually doing. When appropriate, they interview their fellow students, asking them how they felt about the engagement of the lesson. They return to the library and go to the patterns and predictions stage, posting their sticky notes along with the adults on their teams.

The preparation has paid off, and the students' sticky notes are detailed, precise, and focused. They fully participate in the spirited discussions that follow. When, for example, an administrator comments on how a strong pattern around student choice of activity is emerging, Norman, a senior, disagrees: "Choice is overrated. You get the choice between doing a timeline or doing a book review—that's not a big decision. What really matters is authenticity and relevance." Another student, Anne, shares a different point of view: "Choice is one of the most essential things you need for purposeful engagement because with choice comes an opportunity to explore topics of interest to you. Choice in how you learn is also important. Relevancy and choice are the key ingredients to the purposeful engagement tier of the Framework [for Teaching and Learning]."

As they report out, students share what it has been like to talk to their peers during the observations. They are insightful about the evidence collected and the patterns that emerged. George notes, "When I asked students questions, they smiled and were honest with me because I am a student like them." Tom notes that while the rounds teams were in classrooms, students responded differently to their peers than they did to adults. For example, he observed two students engaged in a group task, who told him that they had done this type of work before and were bored. A few minutes later, when an adult observer asked the same students about what they were doing, they gave a shorter and more formal response, describing only the roles they were playing and how they contributed to the lesson.

The animated discussions in the observation groups produce consensus on a number of patterns that are then shared out to the larger group. As the visit winds down (there is not a planned next-level-of-work component because of time constraints), the adults share their appreciation of the student input and their excitement about working together with them. Even though students had taken part in surveys, full-class feedback sessions, panels, and advisory groups that focused on defining engagement for the last two years, there is a palpable sense in the room that history is being made; the principal calls it a "major step on the journey of improving the high school."

When the students are asked what they learned from the visit and what suggestions they could make for improvement of the process, they comment on how valuable it has been for them to see the student-teacher relationship from another perspective. Alexandra notes how watching students learning as an outsider made her see how hard the learning process is, and that "it is OK to be stuck or struggle with a concept or task." The visit has

---

Instructional Rounds in Farmington Public Schools

- Suburban district of seven schools
- Engaged in instructional rounds since 2003
- Nested rounds model (school-based rounds embedded in cross-school and cross-district rounds)
- Grade-level, disciplinary, and/or vertical teams observe and debrief
- Cycles range from five to six times a year to twice a year
- Anchored in district's Framework for Teaching and Learning
- Linked to district-based collaborative inquiry and coaching initiatives

---

helped some of them think differently about their responsibility as students. Duane sums this up: "I thought the teacher had the main role in the learning process, telling us what to do and being responsible for us being engaged. But now I see that it's the students' job. Students need to know if they are engaged or not and take responsibility for being engaged. If we are not, we need to go to the teacher and make suggestions for how we would be engaged—advocate for ourselves." Carl adds, "This was an amazing opportunity. I never saw classes through the eyes of an administrator."

Several express the wish that every student could have the experience they have had today. "It's huge to have students involved in rounds," says Sally. They also have suggestions for improvements of the visit process: one is getting into advanced placement classes; another is making the visits unannounced. And the final student suggestion: "It was good to observe and make patterns, but I would like to come back and talk about how we can make changes and share ideas we have to make improvements." The administrators respond by thanking the students, commending them on their evidence collection as well as reflection and promising to include them in follow-up conversations about school improvement, including the school district's unannounced visits to classrooms alongside teachers and administrators. The superintendent closes the visit, saying that there are important moments in every school district's continuous improvement efforts that stand out. She further states that she considers the first Farmington High School student rounds as one of those moments and believes, "As a result of the student rounds experience, Farmington has reached a more refined level of adult and student partnership in our collective continuous improvement efforts." As the students line up for passes from the principal to allow them to return to their more customary roles in classes, it is clear that they not only contributed to making rounds history today, but that many of them are thinking differently about their roles in the learning process.

BACKGROUND AND CONTEXT

Farmington, a small, relatively affluent school district ten miles southwest of Hartford, Connecticut, was an early adopter in instructional rounds. Its last superintendent, Bob Villanova, was a founding member of the Connecticut Super-intendents' Network, which began conducting interdistrict rounds visits in 2003. He was one of several of the superintendents who, seeing the value of the rounds they were conducting with their peers, brought the practice into their own districts. After a decade of work with standards-based reform, the administrative team was eager to hear about Villanova's experiences with rounds and the way he hoped to use it to make connections between principals and district leaders and classrooms. By 2004, the Farmington District Leadership Council (DLC), comprising all school-based and central office administrators, was conducting rounds. Villanova met with teacher association leaders to expand the purpose of rounds and developed and shared a "theory of action" articulating how rounds would be connected to larger improvement efforts in Farmington. By 2008, several of the principals decided to bring the practice into their own schools. By the time current superintendent Kathleen Greider replaced the retiring Villanova in 2009, most of the seven schools had begun engaging teams of teachers in efforts to "deprivatize practice" by observing in each other's classrooms (see exhibit 5.1).

Farmington has approached its overall improvement efforts in strategic and coherent ways. Key elements include developing and publicizing a "Vision of the Farmington Graduate" that articulates the community's aspirations for their students. (See appendix A at the end of this chapter.) This was developed with student, faculty, administrator, parent, and board of education input and feedback and received formal approval from Farmington's board of education in March 2010.

After approval, it was soon apparent that the role of the student in the learning process needed to change to realize this vision. In June 2010, Greider charged assistant superintendent Kim Wynne with working with a broad-based group of teachers and administrators to develop a "Framework for Teaching and Learning" that outlines what high-quality instruction and learning needs to look like to lead to the desired outcomes for students (see Appendix B at the end of this chapter).

EXHIBIT 5.1

Time line of rounds development in Farmington

- 2004: Administrative rounds; District Leadership Council rounds
- 2008: Deprivatization of practice emerging through teacher to teacher classroom visitations.
- 2009: District Leadership Council rounds include teachers; school-based rounds emerge in schools
- 2009: School-based rounds occurring across schools
- 2010: Vertical rounds initiated
- 2011: Vertical rounds occurring across subject areas and programs
- 2012: School-based rounds with students

Source: Adapted with permission from Kathleen C. Greider, Superintendent, Farmington Public Schools, Connecticut.

The Framework was designed to achieve all elements of the vision of the graduate. Kim Wynne describes this framework as the core of the system's continuous improvement work. Whereas some districts cite multiple strategies and initiatives operating simultaneously, Farmington is intentional and focused on improving instructional practice aligned with the five principles in the Framework.

Other strategies—the strategic use of data, teaming practices, leadership development—are all aimed at the instructional core and ultimately, the vision of the graduate. "Extending our rounds work to include teachers in regularly examining teaching and learning was a natural next step and it has shaped and changed the direction of our professional development and curriculum development significantly," explains Wynne. Grade-level or subject-area teams of teachers began using a rounds-like model the district calls *collaborative inquiry* to visit each other's classrooms and use the evidence to rework lessons and instructional tasks. Two years ago, teachers serving on vertical teams also began using a rounds process. Discipline-specific teachers from all levels K–12 used release time to visit classrooms from elementary to high school over the course of one day, gathering evidence in response to a particular content-specific problem of practice. Because the principles from the Framework anchor all this work, the team's problem of practice is directly connected. Inquiry questions that serve to focus observations sound something like, "We know that students learn best when they make choices about and take responsibility for their own learning goals and progress. What evidence do you see that students are becoming self-directed in their learning?" This kind of question has led to restructuring of assessments and has sparked conversations about the continuum of expectations in every subject area. Instructional improvement is not a mandate in Farmington. High expectations and innovation are hallmarks of a system that has embraced distributed leadership for decades. Teachers are leaders and participants deeply invested in the improvement work of the school and district. The evolution of rounds processes has moved from the administrator to the teacher level and from the district only to school-based practice.

Superintendent Greider stresses that, like many innovations in Farmington, rounds developed organically, with principals learning the practice from each other and through their participation on the District Leadership Council. Although there was no central mandate, the school-based approaches to rounds mirror the DLC processes. As Greider, who also participates in the Connecticut Superintendents' Network, would learn new approaches to the rounds practice there, she would bring them back to Farmington, first to the DLC and ultimately to the schools. She has outlined suggestions for timelines, development of problems of practice, protocols during the visits, and plans for peer follow-up after the visits. She has codified these suggestions as a way to help move the knowledge about when and how to set up and conduct rounds from the central office to the schools. The district has published and distributed a description of the various types of classroom observation protocols and the purposes of each. As the practices expanded, there was a need to clarify the distinct elements of each protocol in an effort to be transparent in their leadership practices (see exhibit 5.2).

Consequently, the protocols used for the school-based visits are closely aligned with one another and with the cross-school rounds approach of the DLC and Connecticut Superintendents' Network practice. Most of the innovation and variation within Farmington has less to do with making changes to the critical aspects of observation and evidence protocols and more to do with the types of rounds, who participates in them, what they focus on, and how tightly they are connected to other improvement efforts. Alicia Bowman, principal of West Woods Upper Elementary School, describes rounds as a tool that can be used for a variety of purposes within the school: "We use rounds as a process to engage in professional learning and support continuous improvement." Several different configurations of school-based rounds exist. Although most such rounds take place primarily within a particular school, they will cross boundaries if needed. For example, after

EXHIBIT 5.2

Learning from practice: Farmington's classroom observation protocols

	Purpose	Process	Other key features
Administrative coaching visits	• To collect evidence relative to the FTL that will inform PD and school development planning • To provide timely and frequent feedback to teachers	• Administrators and department leaders schedule time each week for *observing instruction* across several classrooms. • They record *evidence* relative to particular aspects of the FTL connected to school and/or dept. goals. • Teachers receive *feedback* on an individual basis through conversation or brief notes. • At periodic intervals, *data* from coaching visits is aggregated and shared with the faculty to enhance reflective practice and ongoing *instructional improvement planning*.	• Observations are typically brief—10 to 15 minutes per class and are most often unannounced. • Observers may interact with students without disturbing the lesson in order to gather evidence of the student learning principles. • Resource teachers or other teacher leaders may accompany an administrator to deepen understanding of the FTL as evidenced in a particular discipline.

continued

	EXHIBIT 5.2 (continued)	
	Purpose	*Process*	*Other key features*
Instructional rounds	• To calibrate a common understanding of critical aspects of effective instruction and program coherence • To provide feedback to the school administration or program leadership about the next level of work	• Team selects a *problem of practice* that emanates from student learning data—anecdotal or achievement. • Team *studies the problem* through reading and discussion. • Team *visits multiple classrooms* recording evidence related to the problem of practice. • Team debriefs using a *structured protocol* to move from description to analysis to recommendations for next level of work. • *Feedback* is shared with faculty or other members of the department or team. • An *action plan* is developed and implemented based on the observational analysis and recommendations.	• Instructional rounds may be the work of the DLC, a vertical team, or a department. • Rounds typically involve a group of people visiting multiple classrooms. • Instructional rounds are announced in advance and teachers are asked to participate. • Feedback is focused on instructional or programmatic improvement at scale, not on an individual basis.

	Purpose	Process	Other key features
Collaborative inquiry	• To improve student learning by studying and adjusting instruction • To investigate a challenging learner-centered problem through observation of teaching and learning in the classroom and the evidence in student work • To extend and refine instructional repertoire through collaborative teamwork and action-research	• Team *examines student learning data* (common assessments, interim assessments, student work, to uncover misunderstandings or areas of need. • Team reflects on instructional practice to *formulate an inquiry question that will focus classroom observations.* • Team *observes teaching and learning* collecting and recording evidence. • Team debriefs using a structured protocol to move from description to analysis to *action planning.* • Team *implements the plan and assesses effectiveness* by once again, examining the student work.	• Collaborative Inquiry is team-based and focused on current student learning needs. • Teams repeat cycles of collaborative inquiry throughout the year. • Farmington's model of collaborative inquiry is grounded in the principles and practices of the Data Wise Improvement Process. • By design, EEPD action-research projects include cycles of collaborative inquiry.

continued

EXHIBIT 5.2 (continued)

	Purpose	Process	Other key features
Formal observations	• To supervise and evaluate teachers as a part of district policy • To engage individual teachers in reflective practice focused on the Farmington Teaching Standards • To ensure high quality instruction for every student	• Typically, the teacher meets with the administrator or supervisor for a *pre-observation conference* to discuss the goals and objectives of the lesson. • Administrator and/or supervisor *observe* a full period of instruction and document observation. • During the *post-observation conference* the teacher reflects on the effectiveness of the lesson and engages in a collaborative dialogue about goals for improvement. • A *formal written summary* of the observation, commendations and recommendations is signed by all parties and included in the teacher's file.	• Teachers may ask the administrator or supervisor to notice and record evidence in response to an instructional question. • Teachers can expect to be formally observed two to four times per year depending on tenure status, level of experience and need.
Informal observations	• To supervise and evaluate teaching • To provide focused feedback to teachers	• Administrators or supervisors make unannounced visits to classrooms to observe teaching and learning in connection with the teacher's EEPD project or identified instructional improvement objectives. • Some form of follow-up conversation typically takes place soon after the observation. • The administrator or supervisor may choose to write up a summary of the observation and discussion to include in the teacher's file.	• Informal observations differ from coaching visits in that they are evaluative in nature and focused solely on individual.

Source: Adapted with permission from Kathleen C. Greider, Superintendent, Farmington Public Schools, Connecticut.

doing two internal visits, a science teaching team at West Woods might opt to visit classrooms in another school to help it understand and improve its instruction. At the high school this year, the rounds team crossed another kind of boundary by including students on the observation team to get their voice and input into looking at a challenge area at the school around "purposeful engagement."

All forms of rounds in Farmington are shaped by and interact with the Framework for Teaching and Learning and the district's use of teaming, collaborative inquiry, and a coaching process that has building administrators conducting frequent and brief observations in classrooms:

Teams are at the heart of where the learning, instructional improvement, and use of data takes place. At the elementary schools, these are grade-level teams; in middle school, they are cross-disciplinary teams. At the high school, teams are organized by courses—teachers who teach a common course meet once a week and do their planning, collaborative inquiry, and data work in those teams. There are also vertical teams aligned with subject areas or special topics that cut across the schools and serve as the basis for vertical rounds visits. Farmington invests heavily in the development of teams, team leaders, and their collective ability to focus on instructional improvement, tracking the growth of this central pillar of their theory of action by using a teamwork toolkit, including a teaming rubric. All teams in Farmington use a forty-five-page "Teamwork Toolkit," which includes five teaming rubrics that deal with different aspects of teamwork (e.g., creating norms and team functioning, looking at student work, planning instruction). Exhibit 5.3, excerpted from the teamwork rubric, shows one of the five domains. While the rubric is not specifically purposed to support rounds, it is an important tool to assist teams to function at high levels.

Collaborative inquiry is defined on the Farmington website as "the vital organizing process for the continuous improvement of teaching, learning and leading . . . the ongoing investigation of the effectiveness of instructional practices and leadership practices as they result in improvements in student learning. It involves the disciplined analysis of multiple sources of data on student learning and the examination of the instruction. At the classroom level, teachers study their instructional practices through the examination of lesson design, examination of the tasks and products that students engage in, and observation of teaching and learning."

Coaching calls for principals to be in classrooms one to two days week, doing multiple five- to ten-minute observations, viewing instruction through whatever

EXHIBIT 5.3

Excerpt from Farmington's teamwork rubric (1 of 5 domains)

How will we know if our team is developing the practices that lead to improved student learning?

Purpose: Establishing the Collaborative Team

Guiding question: Are we organized for collaborative work? Do we have a shared commitment to each other and our students?

Level 5	Level 4	Level 3	Level 2	Level 1
• Our team time is organized and efficient. We have established roles and responsibilities to ensure clear communication and focused agendas. • Norms are established and revisited regularly to develop trust and encourage open dialogue. • Protocols are used to balance participation and achieve intended outcomes. • We keep notes to hold ourselves accountable for commitments made at meetings. • We support each other in helping all of the students on our team achieve success.		• Our team meets regularly with a structured agenda. Someone facilitates the meeting. • Norms are set at the beginning of the year, and are rarely revisited or revised to improve team interaction. • Protocols are used occasionally and are helpful in accomplishing specific tasks. • We keep notes and occasionally refer back to them to remember what we were thinking. • We enjoy sharing strategies, materials, ideas, and other resources with team members.		• Our team usually meets together during established team time. The agenda is loosely created by current issues and needs. • Norms are not explicitly stated. Conflict or silence may stand in the way of meaningful dialogue. • Conversations are most often informal and unstructured. • We often leave our meetings with no clear commitments for action steps and/or no written record of next steps. • All or some team members have a "sole practitioner" mind-set. Though they attend meetings and talk about students, curriculum, and teaching, some believe the meetings are a waste of precious time.

Source: Adapted with permission from Kathleen C. Greider, Superintendent, Farmington Public Schools, Connecticut.

specific lens that they are focusing on as a school from the instructional framework. For example, a school might be working on "challenging expectations" or "purposeful engagement." Administrators provide written feedback and personally debrief teachers and also rate the instruction they saw on that particular element on a scale from 1 to 4. Administrators periodically share data with the full faculty focused on the specific framework principle. These ratings are not shared at the individual level but are aggregated for the school. Principals may observe alone or accompanied by other administrators, specialists, or teachers. Farmington is now inviting high school students to join administrators and teachers on coaching visits to focus on the learning side of the Framework for Teaching and Learning.

THE PRACTICE

Before the Visit

Rounds visits need a problem of practice; prepared faculty members who understand what a rounds visit is, why it is done, and how to participate in one; and one or more facilitators to guide the practice. In Farmington, the problem of practice usually connects directly to coaching assessments or other data points (e.g., student work, prior rounds visits, data analyzed as part of collaborative inquiry efforts of the team) and is always anchored to elements of the Framework. Problems of practice usually represent the key work that the school is trying to work on in a given school year and grow out of challenges connected to school development plans. Principal Bowman describes this strong connection in her snapshot description of the rounds improvement cycle: "We focus on a high-leverage strategy, the core improvement strategy that comes from the Framework for Teaching and Learning. The faculty has committed to this focus principle for the year. During coaching visits, administrators collect data on the Framework principle which is then presented to faculty to digest, and together we make adjustments that inform our practice."

Another principal, Renee St. Hilaire, of East Farms Elementary School, very consciously uses data from her coaching observations to help identify barriers or areas of need as part of the problem of practice development that would take place before a full rounds visit. For example, this year she and her colleagues had some concerns that mathematics teachers were using math manipulatives in ways that did not help students get as clear conceptual understanding is they could. To gather more data, she organized a set of coaching visits to math classes to be done by two of the specialists, a teacher, and her. "We wanted to see if this was really a problem of practice. And we needed to see whether this is an area in which teachers need support." She tries to include teachers on these kinds of "pre-problem of practice" assessments both for the increase of teacher buy-in that creates and also for the boost their participation brings to professional development. "Sometimes the teachers come up with some of the ideas for how we can turn around and implement improvements quicker," St. Hilaire notes. "One of the things I struggle with in education is how long it can take to make significant improvement . . . I have found that when teachers are included in on the initial problem-solving process as well as in the professional development, the improvements happen at a much more rapid pace. I end up seeing improvements happening in classrooms the day after teachers have had input into the instructional problem. They start coming up with solutions and it's fantastic." Even if there is only one teacher involved with the observation, St. Hilaire observes that, "because we also employ the team model here, where they have regular team meetings, they are very good at sharing and getting alignment with the curriculum practices." Based on the math observations that St. Hilaire and her team conducted, the school decided to go forward and offer targeted professional development of the use of manipulatives. They will schedule a full rounds visit later in the year to collect evidence about that same problem of practice, and see if the intervention has helped.

St. Hilaire describes how the choice of facilitator for particular rounds depends on the nature and scope of the rounds. She tries to make every DLC visit to East Farms impactful as a school-based visit by including additional teachers on it. She tends to facilitate those visits, as well as the internal rounds that include her specialists. For the grade-level and collaborative inquiry visits, depending on the problem of practice, she looks for the right person to lead them. Facilitating rounds is an important developmental growth opportunity for teachers, says St. Hilaire: "I'm almost always involved in some way or another. But my goal is shared leadership, and I am always looking for everyone to own the work. So while I might be there, I'm trying to model facilitation without me over-facilitating; my ultimate goal empowering and inspiring teachers to lead the work. When she sees likely candidates on a rounds visit, she approaches them and asks: "You're really doing this well. Would you like to help plan the professional development or lead it?"

Teachers learn about the rounds process through active participation and the administrator modeling how to facilitate. In addition, DLC rounds model the rounds process as well as facilitation—this improves the process and facilitation when DLC members return to their schools. St. Hilaire also uses a process where the previous round facilitator (principal) assists the next facilitator with his or her problem of practice development and the facilitation.

At the Visit

Rounds takes many forms in Farmington schools, but always serves as a tool to support the learning and connect to the Framework. Here are several examples of types of visits and what follow-up would take place for each one.

West Woods Upper Elementary School.   The West Woods building administrators and curriculum leaders—the four teachers who are responsible for math, literacy, science, and social studies, along with the special education team leader—meet monthly. There is no set schedule for conducting rounds, but periodically data from the coaching observations or other sources, or the need to dig deeper to understand a stuck point related to the school's focused area of the Framework, will trigger a rounds visit. (Last year this process took place three times.) The rounds process would typically be for half a day, with the seven teachers and administrators splitting into groups to observe five classes for fifteen to twenty minutes each. A recent visit was conducted as a way to take stock at midyear on progress that had been made under the Framework heading of "purposeful engagement." The team was focusing on the student experience in classrooms. It observed in classes across the school, compiled its observation notes, formed the patterns, and then after debriefing among its members brought the data back to the faculty.

Other types of rounds take place within a particular curriculum area. These will typically be led by the curriculum leaders and often without the principal involved. Last year, for example the ten members of the World Language vertical team, led by its director of curriculum, visited classrooms from grades 5 through 12 to examine the progression of speaking skills in the target language. The team was encouraged to share its findings and next level of work with the entire department at a subsequent meeting. Once again, there is no set schedule for when each curriculum vertical team plans to conduct vertical rounds. The visits are typically tied to a content team's examination of achievement data and student work. In this case, the World Language team visits revealed a new understanding of the distinction between speaking and reading aloud and as the follow-up conversations led to widespread engagement and ownership of the revisions of instructional tasks by the department. For an example of a rounds visit focused on reading, see exhibit 5.4.

EXHIBIT 5.4

Schedule for reading rounds

Two years ago at Language Arts Vertical Team rounds, one of the big reveals was that we are very good at creating the scaffold for student learning, but we aren't so good at taking it away. The focus question below beautifully relates to this. We need to figure out how to take that scaffold away so students can display academic and personal excellence, exhibit persistent effort and live as resourceful, inquiring and contributing global citizens.

Focus question:

What evidence is there that students are self-directed and taking ownership of their work and being supported in that process?

Schedule:

Period	Teacher	Room	Class
11:23–12:05	T— and J—	XXX	YYY
12:09–12:51	J—, co-taught with J—	XXX	YYY
12:55–1:37	Reading team	English D	YYY
1:41–2:23	M—	XXX	YYY
2:23–3:00	Rounds participants	XXX	Debrief

- J— will bring inventory of interventions—discuss
- Data collection for intervention effectiveness
- Writing tutorial

Debrief questions to consider:

- Based on the observations, what would a student be able to know and do?
- We wonder about . . .
- What did we see that was a match (that students were being supported in taking ownership and becoming self-directed)?
- What did we see that was a mismatch?
- Based on today's observations, I am going to . . .

Source: Adapted with permission from Kathleen C. Greider, Superintendent, Farmington Public Schools, Connecticut.

West Woods also uses a customized version of rounds for supporting new teachers whenever it becomes apparent that a group of new teachers has a stuck point. A recent example was when teachers were struggling to conduct the tight and focused mini-lesson that is part of reader's workshop. This type of rounds could get triggered by the coaching observation visits done by the principal or by concerns expressed by the mentors for the new teachers or the new teachers themselves. Substitutes would be arranged for a half day for the observation team—which might be three new teachers, their mentors, and the literacy specialist. (If the teacher leaders involved are familiar with facilitating the rounds practice, principal Alicia Bowman will typically stay out of this.) The classroom visits will be targeted—timed so that the observers will see mini-lessons from their peers who are more experienced with them. The usual process is used—sticky notes, patterns, predictions—leading to next-level-of-work suggestions. Although it would appear that the biggest learning for this sort of rounds is for the observers, Bowman notes the value for the teachers who have been observed of getting feedback on their own classroom practice, and for the literacy specialist's understanding of implementation on that particular skill in the school. And while in one sense the next-level-of-work suggestions at the end of the visit can be very personal, particularly for the teachers who have been observing, Bowman has found that the suggestions are almost always applicable not only to the new teachers, but to tenured teachers as well: "As a community of professional learners, we are all trying to improve our instructional practice along a continuum. So when the feedback and next level of work are summarized, we ensure that it is in a format that can be easily understood by all and share it at a literacy meeting or perhaps at a faculty meeting as appropriate."

After this type of visit, the new teachers are supported by their mentors or literacy specialist in implementing any of the key ideas they've learned; the personalized next-level-of-work suggestions may become part of their individual improvement plans or the skill sets that they're working on. In addition, because the principal and assistant principal are frequently in classrooms for coaching observations, the administration will have a very good idea of what is being implemented and what is not. If a new teacher is not implementing the improvements, the mentors do not get involved in any sort of evaluative way, and the onus shifts to the administration for follow-up and support.

East Farms Elementary School.   In addition to five or six curriculum specialist rounds a year, similar to those conducted at West Woods, East Farms supports grade-level collaborative inquiry two times a year, where each grade-level team has half-day substitutes to allow members to interact with each other in ways that will support their learning. The team meets the day before to identify a problem of practice—typically targeted to the larger school focus on the Framework. The collaborative inquiry can take a variety of forms. The following example has some rounds-like qualities and also some qualities of lesson study.

In 2012, the five first-grade teachers decided to focus on ways they could help their students develop persistence in working on word problems. They decided to make some plans for innovative ways to approach this and then have one teacher teach a lesson incorporating these changes while the rest watched. They would then take a forty-five-minute debrief to reflect on the instruction and make suggestions for improvement. Then a second teacher would teach the lesson incorporating the improvements, and the group would debrief again. The teachers kept experimenting by changing the amount of scaffolding and then watched the results for the students. Since they ran out of time in their half-day cycle, they agreed to do this three more times in the other teachers' rooms (either observing in person or using videotape) over the next few days. They then used their teaching team meeting to follow it up (to debrief, figure out what they had learned, and identify their next level of work) and to be prepared to share it with the rest of the faculty. Principal Renee St. Hilaire wanted them to bring their findings back to the whole faculty because she sees a wonderful opportunity in this work to help the teachers at all the grade levels make connections between their individual learning and what they and others have been seeing on school- and district-based rounds around the same issue. For St. Hilaire, "It's all the same. It has to do with the instructional decisions that we make both in setting up the task and in the facilitation." She goes on to describe the connections between this rounds-like activity and rounds:

> It's more like lesson study, not exactly like diagnosing but again improving teaching and learning practices. Some of them have chosen the problem of practice because they have been a part of the district and the school rounds and so they know how to do it. This is a big change of culture. The first time that I saw them do collaborative inquiry, I was worried. It kind of went like this: they would watch one teacher teach, they would say, "This is great and here's why." And it was all about living in the "world of nice," and they weren't really looking for evidence or being critical or saying "What if . . . ?" There wasn't that mind-set. Rounds has also contributed to a sense of risk taking with not everybody feeling like they have to do the same thing in the same way in their team time.

After the Visit

Just as each example of the rounds described above started in some key way with the Framework and with the specific focus that the school was working on, each of them ends in the same way by bringing the learning back to the team and to the faculty. See exhibit 5.5 to see the follow-up notes taken from the Reading Team visit outlined in exhibit 5.4. In addition, a week later, a summary of the debriefing highlights section was sent to the superintendent, principals of the involved schools, and curriculum coordinators.

EXHIBIT 5.5

Excerpted notes from reading rounds

The original document includes specific comments about what was observed in each classroom, identified by subject, teacher(s) and period. This excerpt includes a sample of one such set of observation notes, with teacher names removed.

Grades 5–12 reading and writing intervention pathway team rounds
Farmington High School

Focus question:

What evidence is there that students are self-directed and taking ownership of their work and being supported in that process?

Sample classroom observation notes

Period X observation: Grade X, co-taught English XX (50% of the students have IEPs)
Teachers: X and Y

- Lesson components: (1) words of the day; (2) read "Warp Speed" (we, me, you); (3) paired discussion; (4) assign written response for homework

- Task: Annotate the story based on the questions you will have to answer for homework tonight.

- After students had used the guided questions to help annotate the text, the teacher stated that these were intended to help students find deeper meaning in the text.

- There were about 16 students in this class. A regular education teacher led the instruction and the special education teacher circulated providing individual support. Students were seated in a semicircle facing the teacher who moved between the front and the center of the room.

continued

EXHIBIT 5.5 *(continued)*

Debrief highlights:

- We should use the same mnemonic for written responses from grades 5–12. We need further discussion to decide which one to use. Should we use EATS or 5 Es or ASEC? To be determined . . .

- Many of the same students who were in Reading Acceleration in grade 5 are still being assigned to interventions in high school. Should we be concerned about this, or should we accept that some students are likely to need tiered support throughout their school career?

- J——, T——, and M—— have developed a "benchmark" assessment that includes both fiction and nonfiction selections. The text is grade-level text found on Story Island. Teachers are using a rubric to evaluate the work. Students are encouraged to reflect on their own progress and set personal improvement goals.

- Tenth-grade students have read two books in class so far this year. Is this enough? Do they have time to read books at their "just right" level or are they typically expected to work only on these challenging texts?

- How much of what is learned in the intervention setting is transferred to other settings? Teachers are seeing some evidence of this; i.e., one student borrowed a list of sentence starters to use for a social studies writing project.

- We decided to have a common way of naming reading interventions from grades 5–12. We will call a Tier 3 intervention class "Literacy Workshop" and a Tier 2 class will be known as "Literacy Lab." B—— and D—— will talk to their respective guidance departments immediately to make this clarification.

- J—— explained her role in supporting the 5–8 reading and writing interventions. She will visit IAR and FHS teachers to ask for help with program descriptions sometime in the winter.

- The team will discuss progress monitoring and data collection systems during this year's meetings. We need to develop a consistent and easily understood system.

- We brainstormed what we would like to see across all FHS grade 5–12 literacy interventions during our visits. We might use this list to guide our collaborative inquiry rounds in the future:
  ○ Increasingly rigorous performance expectations from grade to grade
  ○ Independent application of skills that have been taught (should we also explore whether we are teaching explicitly for transfer of learning to other settings?)
  ○ Common language/vocabulary across all classrooms
  ○ Time with eyes on text—reading time
  ○ Books at "just right" levels available in the classroom
  ○ Electronic devices/readers

 We will conduct our next rounds on Thursday, January 31, 2013 at IAR from 11:30 AM–3:30 p.m.
 D—— will look at the Chris Tovani video "Talk to Me" to see if we might want to view it together at some point.

Source: Adapted with permission from Kathleen C. Greider, Superintendent, Farmington Public Schools, Connecticut.

The findings from a rounds visit would typically be brought back to the faculty to initiate a reflective process—one that always comes back to the Framework principle of the year. In the West Woods curriculum team example that looked closely at students, the underlying topic was "purposeful engagement." At the faculty meeting, the teachers would be asked to look at the information that is being shared, describe what they notice in it, and think about what implications it has for the school, for themselves as individuals, and for their teams. They would also be asked to consider what follow-up would need to be done over the next week, over the next month, and over the next year. These discussions after rounds visits provide opportunities for the school revisit to their vision of exactly what, for instance, "purposeful engagement" should look like in an upper elementary school and to tweak that and refine it in light of the new learning.

Alicia Bowman describes herself as "trying to establish a culture of continuous improvement characterized by collective ownership and mutual accountability." Every team in the school has a collaborative goal, which is a part of the evaluation process and connected to the schoolwide focus. Bowman suggests to teachers: "Make a commitment relative to our findings, something that you want to do as a team before next faculty meeting and then come back and tell us about it." She continues,

> Or I might ask the team leaders to bring back their artifacts and be ready to share strategies that their team has tried at the next leadership team meeting. Or tell a team of teachers, "We'll discuss their commitments at our midyear meeting and I'll be interested to find out what progress you made." One of the strengths of having a common focus [by working as a school on one identified element of the Framework] is that we are all heading in the same direction with the same goal. It is more likely that I'll see the follow-up and the follow-through because without a clearly articulated improvement strategy, people feel splintered, unsure about how to focus their efforts.

The leadership actions that are described by both Bowman and St. Hilaire reflect the modeling that has occurred at the DLC level through rounds, collaborative coaching, and case studies on teaming, data collection, leadership development, and twenty-first-century leadership practice.

In addition to this work on individual and collective accountability for teams, the findings from the rounds are also used to shape the bigger schoolwide planning and accountability documents. Superintendent Greider describes how the district has moved from school development plans that are long narratives to ones that are mostly charts and action plans that can be very responsive to data and ideas that are coming from rounds or coaching. Based on new information, principals can put all the professional development support systems into play, asking, according to Greider, "What are we going to do differently with our leadership teams, our literacy specialists; what about professional development at our next faculty meeting; what will I focus on in my next coaching visits?" She adds,

> Rounds has a ripple effect on all the systems that we use in the district. With formats and resources that people can use, it brings simplicity to a very complex process. Rounds, as it has evolved, changes everything. It's not changing the focus of the development plan because the focus is around the Framework for Teaching and Learning, which links to our district goals and vision of the graduate. But what we had planned at the beginning of year may change. Rounds provides a periodic dipstick to inform the schools and district where we are and what we need to do next.

Improvement discussions between principals and Greider occur regularly and are grounded in evidence Greider spends one day per week in classrooms conducting coaching visits with principals, literacy and math specialists, and teachers. This provides multiple opportunities to analyze instruction as well as the school's development plan work. These conversations help her stay connected to the work and promote close monitoring and adjustments to the school development plan because coaching, rounds, collaborative inquiry, and ongoing data collection inform the school's next level of work on a regular basis. She states, "I'm okay with the principal who says, 'I did not get to everything that we planned to get to in our school development plan because rounds informed the school to go deeper in a particular area,' or 'We were able to do more because rounds provided evidence that the work was well underway and we could move at a faster rate.'"

CONNECTIONS TO SCHOOL AND DISTRICT IMPROVEMENT PRACTICES

In Farmington Public Scools, the different pieces of the puzzle are closely integrated. School-based rounds, vertical rounds, and District Leadership Council rounds all connect to each other as well as to the frequent coaching observations, the team structure, and collaborative inquiry to fit together like parts of a strategic learning organization. Three particularly strong connections are the nested quality of the different levels of rounds practice, the back-and-forth between the rounds practice and the coaching/observation practice (all guided by the focusing of the Framework), and the symbiotic nature of rounds and teaming.

The seventeen-member District Leadership Council (comprised of school-based and central office administrators) conducts cross-school rounds. In addition, schools that are hosting a particular DLC visit may include several teachers as part of the visiting team. Each of Farmington's seven schools can expect a DLC visit roughly every year and a half. (See exhibit 5.6 for the District Leadership Team visit preparation and follow-up timeline.)

Most principals have become adept at building on those visits to maximize the impact at their schools. Renee St. Hilaire describes how, well before the visit, she brings together the core group of faculty—those who will be visited, as well as the several she will have on the visiting team with the DLC. Together, they refine their problem of practice and identify particular areas that they want feedback on. Aware that sometimes the observers will come from other schools and different grade levels (and not know as much about the particular kind of teaching they will be observing) the host teachers try to be specific about the observable indicators that will be helpful to them as the visiting group gathers its data.

After the visitors have come and gone and have left their observations and suggestions, the principal reconvenes the team, including the teachers who had been on the visit as well as the teachers whose classrooms had been visited. They look at what each of the six visit team groups have given them for evidence, patterns, predictions and next level of work and decide which of these makes the most sense for the school to follow up on. They then bring it all—the posters with the sticky notes and the evidence—to the whole faculty. Faculty members are encouraged to take the time to read the data from the visit and to make their own interpretations—to think about what the implications of those patterns and predictions are. For the principal, this is an important part of developing real buy-in on the part of the entire faculty, not just those who have been visited. The message she tries to send is, "The outcomes, and the celebrations, and the suggestions for improvement that come from the rounds visit are reflections of the whole school. This is how *we* did and this is where *we* need to go next." This faculty meeting will be led by the teachers who are involved in the visit—the observers as well as the observed—and will lead to the next level of work commitments that the faculty as a whole will be making for their follow-up. Often this takes the form of making revisions to the professional development plan that the school has sketched out for the year to target particular skills connected to this identified next level of work. The principal will then look for some teachers who are skilled and interested in stepping up to help develop and deliver that professional development.

EXHIBIT 5.6

District leadership team visit preparation and follow-up timeline

2 weeks ahead	1 week ahead	DLC visit	Post-visit activities	DLC follow-up activities
Participating teachers and principal develop a problem of instructional practice.	Article sent out ahead that grounds the DLC with the problem of instructional practice	1. DLC norms review 2. Background • Problem of instructional practice and its grounding in the framework, school development plan and theory of action • Article discussion • View team video "Does the work of the team affect the work in the classroom?"	Principal and participating teachers plan the faculty debrief.	Principal to report at a subsequent DLC: "What were the themes or patterns that the school embraced as meaningful and influenced the next level of work for the school?" "Did these experiences lead to changes in my TOA?"

2 weeks ahead	1 week ahead	DLC visit	Post-visit activities	DLC follow-up activities
Principal colleague makes a pre-visit to review the preparatory work with the principal and, possibly, the participating teachers	Host prepares introduction to DLC visit. Link to school development plan and theory of action.	Observations: 3–4 classrooms per team (15 minutes per classroom)	School team shares the ideas from the next level of the work. What themes are meaningful to the faculty? How and when to proceed?	DLC members to reflect: "What are the implications for my leadership practices, for theory of action, for future DLC learning?
Video practice for teachers who do not have experience viewing instruction and describing it.	Create a video of a team at work.	Debrief: • Descriptive • Analysis • Patterns • Next level of work	Principal colleague makes a post-visit to discuss the status of the school follow-up plan.	Generate statements to share with the faculty as initial feedback.

Source: Adapted with permission from Kathleen C. Greider, Superintendent, Farmington Public Schools, Connecticut.

Although DLC rounds occur in one school, the next level of work for that school has implications for all seven schools because of the strong coherence created by the district goals, vision of the graduate, and Framework for Teaching and Learning. So, when the next level of work is shared at a DLC rounds visit, all members of the council are gaining insights that they bring back to their teams and schools to inform their improvement work.

There is a tremendous back-and-forth between rounds practice and the more frequent shorter observations that are being done—mostly by administrators, but with some teacher involvement—under the heading of "coaching." These very frequent data points of what is going on in classrooms serve both as an early identification system for problems of practice and as a monitoring system for looking at improvement after rounds and any adjustment to instructional practice have been made. The rounds practice does not sit in isolation in the schools, but is woven together with other practices, all of which are tied to the instructional framework (see exhibit 5.7).

Superintendent Greider sees powerful connections between rounds and instructional improvement. Even though principals had begun talking about school-based rounds before her superintendency, she immediately saw the value in it and encouraged this next level of innovative work. Since DLC rounds would only take place every six to eight weeks across the entire district, launching school-based work would increase the frequency of feedback and reflection. But, she notes, "The real power in rounds is that teachers who participate raise questions about practice that would not have come up otherwise in team discussion. We are a district that is committed to team structures and team learning, but these areas of improvement may not come up without going into classrooms and actually viewing practice. Otherwise, there are gaps that may occur within team improvement discussions. Going into classrooms helps fill those gaps and allows people to bring back what they learn in rounds—to have it come back to the team. Teachers have come to understand that they have to analyze practice and that it raises the level of instruction for all students when they analyze practice on a regular basis."

This approach is consistent with Farmington's learning theory of action that implicates every member of the teaching faculty. A systemic approach to capacity building is articulated in the district's "Learning 2.0" document, which states, "One of the central leadership functions and challenges is to unleash the collective capacity of our teaching faculty and staff to its greatest potential using collaborative inquiry processes. This requires us to develop a deeper vision for team learning, which in turn requires team leaders to develop the facilitation and planning

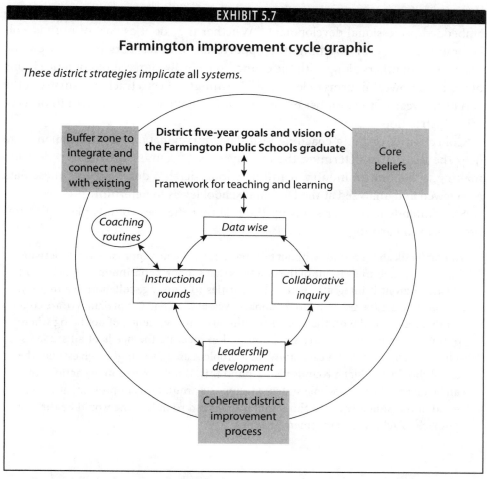

EXHIBIT 5.7

Farmington improvement cycle graphic

These district strategies implicate all systems.

Source: Adapted with permission from Kathleen C. Greider, Superintendent, Farmington Public Schools, Connecticut.

skills that support the deep engagement of faculty in the examination of instructional practices."

The teacher evaluation model used in Farmington also aligns with this theory. Teachers are required to work with a team to develop an action-research project annually. Professional learning goals arise from these projects, and teachers are provided with resources, consultation with experts, release time, and other forms of support for their continued growth and development.

The rounds process itself is seen by the superintendent as a key form of job embedded professional development: "Whether they do it as part of rounds, collaborative inquiry, or coaching, the opportunity that teachers have to view the instruction of others along with the chance to have discourse about practice is one of the most powerful forms of learning." Farmington keeps track in a survey at the end of the year of the number of opportunities that teachers have had to observe other instruction.

Collection of ongoing coaching visit data, survey data, and achievement data help the district to determine the effectiveness of rounds, data-driven decision making, collaborative inquiry, teaming, and leadership development. These data are viewed and analyzed at the DLC and school levels to determine progress.

Superintendent Greider sums up the role that she sees rounds playing in improvement in Farmington:

> You can't talk about rounds without talking about a systems approach to districtwide improvement. Rounds is one of the practices that supports continuous improvement in Farmington. It integrates with others. It ties to teaming, collaborative inquiry, case studies, action research, professional development, and use of data. We are constantly preoccupied with the idea of continuous improvement—of not being where we want to be because we are so committed to meeting the needs of all students. When the DLC looks at a case study [of a problem area], we might suggest that the school should conduct a rounds visit around this. But it's one of many actions that can be taken. There is a whole system of supports around this improvement work. I would never want anyone to think that rounds and rounds alone would be the one approach to achieve improvement at scale.

APPENDIX A: CHAPTER 5

Vision of the Farmington graduate

Farmington Graduates: Reaching global standards of achievement, leadership, and citizenship

Farmington Public Schools' Graduates *will acquire an understanding of the essential knowledge and skills in the core academic disciplines and develop the thinking and learning skills needed to meet the challenges of local, national and global citizenship in a rapidly changing world.*

Critical thinking and reasoning

Students access, interpret, analyze, and evaluate ideas and information, draw evidence-based conclusions, synthesize new learning with prior knowledge, and reflect critically on learning.

Students who demonstrate critical thinking and reasoning skills . . .

- Ask questions to revise or adjust understanding
- Use critical reading strategies to develop meaning from text
- Support arguments with clear and compelling evidence
- Make connections between new information and prior knowledge
- Analyze and evaluate data to draw conclusions
- Recognize values, beliefs, bias and perspective
- Acknowledge different opinions to foster new insight
- Notice patterns and analyze cause and effect

Communication and collaboration

Students participate effectively in a variety of teams, actively listen and respond to the ideas of others, share responsibility for outcomes, articulate ideas clearly in multiple formats and use technology tools to enhance communication.

Students who effectively communicate and collaborate . . .

- Write and speak clearly for a variety of purposes
- Demonstrate an awareness of audience and adjust style and tone accordingly
- Use language effectively to enhance meaning and impact
- Use a variety of technology tools to enhance communication
- Access diverse perspectives and expertise to accomplish a goal
- Establish and adhere to group norms that facilitate effective performance

continued

APPENDIX A: CHAPTER 5 *(continued)*

- Listen to and value the contributions of others on the team
- Adapt to and perform a variety of roles and responsibilities within a group

Problem solving and innovation

Students identify problems, analyze data, ask questions, utilize a variety of resources, think flexibly, make connections and seek practical, innovative and entrepreneurial solutions to a variety of problems.

Students who are problem solvers and innovators . . .

- Notice, examine, and reframe problems
- Ask questions and brainstorm ideas
- Detect patterns and anomalies in data
- Embrace contradictions and divergent ideas
- Relate the apparently unrelated
- Produce novel and creative solutions and products
- Take risks and go beyond conventional parameters
- Employ strategic processes to learn from success and failure

Self-direction and resourcefulness

Students explore interests, take initiative, set goals, demonstrate persistent effort, adapt to change with resiliency, and exhibit ethical leadership and responsible citizenship.

Self-directed and resourceful students . . .

- Act on curiosity and pursue interests
- Manage time and organize tasks
- Work to overcome obstacles and learn from mistakes
- Seek feedback and new resources to accomplish a goal
- Reflect on learning experiences
- Transfer knowledge and skills from one context to another
- Find opportunities for civic engagement and leadership
- Make ethical, responsible decisions

Source: Adapted with permission from Kathleen C. Greider, Superintendent, Farmington Public Schools, Connecticut.

Farmington framework for teaching and learning

Principle #1: Active learning community

Students learn best when they have a sense of belonging to a positive learning community in which they have regular opportunities to work collaboratively.

Teachers...

- Organize the classroom environment with clearly established routines and behavioral expectations
- Create effective systems to hold students accountable for individual and group responsibilities
- Model thinking and share learning as a member of the classroom community
- Provide direct instruction and guided practice in the skills and dispositions of effective collaborative work
- Encourage questions, nurture multiple points of view and value intellectual risk-taking
- Facilitate student to student discourse, developing effective communications skills
- Structure opportunities for students to share work publicly
- Promote learning through engagement with others as mentors and critics

Students...

- Establish and reflect on classroom and small group norms for respectful behavior and effective communication
- Participate actively in discussions and collaborative tasks
- Speak and write clearly to communicate with others
- Exchange meaningful and constructive feedback
- Clarify ideas by asking questions, listening to others
- Investigate and appreciate multiple points of view
- Share their work publicly and engage in dialogue about process and product

Teachers...

- Organize the classroom environment with clearly established routines and behavioral expectations
- Create effective systems to hold students accountable for individual and group responsibilities
- Model thinking and share learning as a member of the classroom community
- Provide direct instruction and guided practice in the skills and dispositions of effective collaborative work

continued

- Encourage questions, nurture multiple points of view and value intellectual risk-taking
- Facilitate student to student discourse, developing effective communications skills
- Structure opportunities for students to share work publicly
- Promote learning through engagement with others as mentors and critics

Principle #2: Challenging expectations

Students learn best when they understand performance expectations and are individually supported in meeting challenging standards.

Teachers . . .
- Maintain high expectations for all students
- Communicate learning goals clearly
- Anticipate misconceptions and connect new learning to prior knowledge
- Articulate performance expectations using rubrics and exemplars of quality work
- Provide timely and specific feedback to students
- Differentiate instruction using a variety of resources, materials and grouping strategies responsively
- Design opportunities for students to demonstrate understanding in a variety of ways

Students . . .
- Ask questions to clarify expectations and learning goals
- Use and maintain organizational systems to support academic achievement
- Persist in the face of challenging learning tasks
- Evaluate and revise work using rubrics, models, and feedback
- Overcome obstacles to understanding by seeking teacher or peer support
- Seek new resources and strategies for learning

Principle #3: Meaningful knowledge

Students learn best when they see content as meaningful and organized around big ideas and questions and can transfer learning to new contexts.

Teachers . . .
- Provide a clear purpose for learning and focus instruction on essential understandings and essential questions
- Make explicit connections between students' prior knowledge to new learning

- Link content knowledge to students' personal experiences, real world events, and other disciplines
- Develop tasks that require students to synthesize, transfer and apply their knowledge and skills to new situations
- Use data to engage students in analytical and critical thinking about conceptual ideas
- Expect students to support thinking with clear and compelling evidence

Students . . .

- Look for connections between what they are learning and what they already know
- Articulate the purpose of their learning to themselves and others
- Transfer learning skills and knowledge from one context to another
- Recognize bias, values and beliefs and understand their impact on knowledge
- Access, analyze and create data to understand conceptual ideas
- Support thinking with clear, logical and relevant evidence

Principle #4: Purposeful engagement

Students learn best when they are actively engaged in authentic learning tasks and given opportunities to construct meaning and develop understanding.

Teachers . . .

- Structure learning tasks that engage students in authentic work of the discipline
- Develop inquiry-oriented lessons in response to essential questions
- Pose complex, intriguing and challenging problems for students to solve
- Stimulate critical and creative thinking and model active listening
- Use multimedia and technology tools to enhance learning outcomes
- Seek and provide real audiences for student work
- Act as coaches, facilitators, and guides to promote engagement and develop leadership in students

Students . . .

- Actively seek answers to their own questions and explore their interests
- Hypothesize, analyze, question, and evaluate ideas within the work of the discipline
- Accept opportunities to assume partnership and leadership roles in the classroom
- Take initiative to bring interesting ideas and resources into the classroom community
- Think critically and use reasoning skills to develop understanding

continued

APPENDIX B: CHAPTER 5 *(continued)*

• Think creatively and use problem solving skills to develop innovative ideas

Principle #5: Individual responsibility

Students learn best when they make choices about and take responsibility for their own learning goals and progress.

Teachers . . .

• Design learning tasks that require students to be self-directed, make choices and manage time effectively to achieve their learning goals
• Structure group tasks to ensure individual and collective accountability
• Plan for regular opportunities for student reflection through discussion and writing
• Foster a growth mindset helping students to see mistakes as learning opportunities
• Celebrate resiliency and resourcefulness in the face of setbacks or obstacles

Students . . .

• Evaluate the quality of their performances / work products
• Set learning goals and reflect on progress
• Learn from their own mistakes and develop new strategies
• Advocate for themselves by asking for help when needed
• Learn to become self-directed to make choices that match interests and learning needs
• Assume responsibility for good work habits
• Develop leadership skills in areas of interest

Source: Adapted with permission from Kathleen C. Greider, Superintendent, Farmington Public Schools, Connecticut.

CHAPTER 6

Rounds Reconsidered in an Independent School
Ballarat Clarendon College

There was an air of concern in the room as the Ballarat Clarendon College rounds planning team gathered in the office. As the students departed for the long summer break, it seemed like a good time to "push the pause button" and take stock of the impacts of the enormous investment BCC had made in the instructional rounds process over the previous eighteen months. Two teams sent off to the United States to learn rounds at the Harvard Graduate School of Education; forty staff members—almost half the staff—involved in observations. The effort and commitment required to drive rounds forward was significant. What did the school have to show for it? Could it be sustained? Had the team somehow lost its way, focusing too much on getting the rounds process "right" but losing sight of its purpose and connection to improvement? Was it losing momentum—was that sense of traction gained in the earliest phases slipping away?

Steven Belcher, the head of curriculum for the senior school, held the "map"—the "Plan for College Improvement"—in front of him. The group became quiet as he started the discussion: "We have so many levers representing the 'how' of our delivery on the improvement plan. Instructional rounds is one of those. It's starting to feel like an add-on rather than an integral cog in the improvement mechanism."

"I agree," added Reid Smith, his counterpart at the middle school. "I worry about continuing to commit the same level of intellectual and emotional energy that we have been. We're trading on the good will and trust of our colleagues. We need to sure we know which drivers will help us move forward. Is rounds producing the learning we expected it to?"

"We haven't done enough around the next level of work yet. We have removed the work so far from the classroom that it's hard to connect back. We need to take the time to build capacity of the participants to learn. I don't think we're seeing the learning at the moment." This was from Laura Brady, who had been instrumental in supporting and guiding teachers as they learned to make nonjudgmental observations in their colleagues' classrooms, worked collaboratively to identify patterns, and struggled to synthesize these into the critical next level of work.

"Instructional rounds has the potential to build the capacity of all teachers," said Nick Stansbie, one of the rounds facilitators. "We need to make a decision about how it fits."

"Are we going about rounds in the wrong way? It's not a project on its own. It's designed to support our improvement strategy. It's not an improvement agenda. We need to attach it to something." Reid's contribution caused a pause in the discussion.

"We are involved in so many improvement efforts. How does rounds connect with the work of the English team in Writing, for example? I'm not sure that it does," added Caitlin Pohl, another facilitator.

"Which improvement process is rounds connected to, then?" her colleague Shaune Moloney asked.

Steven looked around the table: "We're currently trying to get people to focus on so many things. I'm concerned that people will disconnect from instructional rounds because they have got nothing out of it. We need to alter our course slightly. Motivation is decreasing and the wheels are slipping."

"We have practiced and rehearsed the process. We don't need to do that anymore. So, what are we trying to improve? What could we attach it to? We can't scramble around looking for improvement projects," Laura continued.

"Let's scale back until we can clarify and focus," offered Steven.

"We need to spend some time thinking about the next level of work. Let's pause and think. The decision needs to be made by the whole group; we all need to take responsibility. We should take a break from observations and consolidate," agreed Reid.

Nick had been thinking. "Have we actually thought deeply enough about the kinds of support that our teachers need to move instruction to 'the next level'? We know this phase is difficult. It is much easier to talk in broad brush strokes and to grab loose concepts like 'formative assessment' and 'questioning' than it is to drill down to the level of specificity and detail that would actual require real work from us all."

"It's the next level of work that's bothering us, but maybe we are actually disconnecting earlier in the process," commented Caitlin as she flicked through her copy of *Instructional Rounds in Education*. "When we go through the prediction phase, do we ever to ask the

---

Instructional Rounds in Ballarat Clarendon College

- Large independent school in an urban setting, serving students ages 3–18
- Engaged in instructional rounds since 2010, with pause to take stock and tune in 2012
- Stand-alone rounds model
- Self-nominated teams of teachers and leaders observe and debrief
- Rounds process is "stretched out" so the parts of the observation and debrief cycle are not done in one day; cycle repeats every six weeks
- Anchored in collaboratively defined problems of practice
- Linked to individually developed theories of action

---

critical question—what causes the learning we want to see? If we don't go deeply enough, then we couldn't expect to . . . —and she reads—'identify the potential areas for improvement and get clues into how these areas could be improved, including the specific moves that a teacher could use.'"

Heads were nodding. The team had come to an *aha* moment. Shaune voiced the question that was on everyone's mind: "Are we avoiding the real work?"

BACKGROUND AND CONTEXT

Ballarat Clarendon College is an independent coeducational school situated in regional Victoria, Australia. It is about an hour and a half's drive northwest of Melbourne, population of about 100,000. BCC enrolls 1,300 students, ages three through eighteen, including 150 boarders who come from country areas of Victoria and New South Wales. The school, with a staff of over 100 full-time equivalents, is about to celebrate its 150th year and recently earned recognition as the top regional school in Australia. Students are predominantly white, with 90 percent native English speakers. The student attendance rate sits at 94 percent, and 97 percent of students study at university after leaving BCC.

The school works hard to keep in touch with what is going on around the world, especially concerning new ideas related to school improvement, change management, and strategies for instruction. In 2010, it realized that its improvement work had taken hold in different ways across the school, and despite all its efforts, it still had more variability across classrooms than it wanted—a greater difference existed between classrooms at the one school than between schools. When members of its leadership team staff read *Instructional Rounds in Education*, they saw rounds as a way of breaking down the atomization of individual classrooms and facilitating the sharing of best practice across the school. The team, consisting of deputy principal Jan McClure, head of curriculum for the middle school Reid Smith, head of curriculum for the senior school Steven Belcher, and head of literacy Jennifer McGie summarizes what their thinking was at that point: "We had begun the work of building a coherent practice of professional culture, but only at the surface level. What we hoped to learn from the [rounds] work was how to increase or deepen the level of coherence around classroom practice. We also wanted to learn more about how to develop the common language about instructional practice. Additionally, we needed to better understand accountability at the classroom level."[1]

After sending the first team to the Rounds Institute at the Harvard Graduate School of Education in 2010, the school developed a plan to implement upon the team's return to Australia. Because it was one of just a few independent schools (as opposed to multischool districts) at the Institute, BCC needed to make adaptations in the practice and in the protocols to make rounds work. It started with a pilot effort as a "proof of concept." Eight middle school English teachers observed each other's classes to practice the process and make initial observations and patterns. This was mainly for practice. After the team reported that the process worked smoothly and was manageable, Ballarat expanded the pilot to other volunteers later the same year. It introduced the basic concepts of instructional rounds to the entire staff, invited questions, and asked for teachers to volunteer to participate (heads of department, who have both teaching and administrative responsibilities, were required to be participants). Seventeen staff volunteered and began conducting rounds, with teachers, Heads of Department, and Heads of School involved as equals. A major part of the focus was on learning the details of the rounds practice. Staff would discuss their observations directly after completing their observations in their small teams, so the leader of the observation group—typically someone who had been trained at Harvard or during the first pilot phase—could give feedback on the types of observations that were being made by participants. More of their focus was on getting the rounds practice "right" (e.g., using nonjudgemental statements) than on getting to strong or impactful patterns. During this phase, teachers could opt out of having their classrooms observed.

THE PRACTICE

Before the Visit

By the end of 2010 and moving into 2011, the school scaled up to include around forty self-nominated staff members. They worked in teams of eight, with all classes open for observation. Rounds was facilitated by six of the eight staff who had completed the rounds course at Harvard (the principal and deputy principal did not facilitate). By this point, a number of the teachers were familiar with the rounds from earlier versions.

During this iteration of rounds, Ballarat "borrowed" a problem of practice from one of the schools that team members had visited while at Harvard. It adapted it to focus on the tasks that BCC students were being asked to do and the extent to which students were getting opportunities to practice higher-order thinking skills like analyzing, evaluating, and creating. Near the end of 2011, the rounds planning team decided to have all visits focus on the same problem of practice. After the facilitators developed an initial draft, they e-mailed it to the participants to provide feedback and refinement. They ended up with a problem of practice that focused not only on task but on the degree to which staff were using information/data from the classroom to inform their teaching:

> We are not consistently using information/data from the classroom to inform our teaching. This affects the level of the tasks, the challenge of teacher questions and the level of mastery students are able to demonstrate.
>
> **Focus questions:**
> - What is the task?
> - What key strategies are being used and how are they being used to adapt teaching and learning to meet student needs? How are students taking some responsibility for the monitoring of their own learning?

See Exhibit 6.1 for the five key strategies for instructional improvement Ballarat was trying to weave into instruction.

At the Visit

In a modification of rounds to better fit a school-based setting (and to eliminate the need for substitutes) BCC "stretched" the rounds process out. Observers would see three classes in a period as well as conduct a debriefing, so each classroom would be observed for approximately fifteen to twenty minutes. Each group spent a period a week for six weeks observing, and would then gather in one room to share observations and produce patterns.

EXHIBIT 6.1

Five key strategies for instructional improvement

- Clarifying, understanding, and sharing learning intentions (curriculum philosophy)
- Engineering effective classroom discussions, tasks, and activities that elicit evidence of learning (classroom discourse, interactive whole-class teaching)
- Providing feedback that moves learners forward (feedback)
- Activating students as learning resources for one another (collaborative learning, reciprocal teaching, peer assessment)
- Activating students as owners of their own learning (metacognition, motivation, interest, attribution, self-assessment)

Source: Adapted with permission from Jan McClure, Deputy Principal, Ballarat Clarendon College, Victoria, Australia.

The patterns collected from visits included:

- There were large differences in the way content was addressed between one classroom and the classroom next door, despite coplanning and discussion.
- Teachers were doing most of the work in classes.
- Students could articulate the *what* (sometimes) but often not the *why* of what they are doing.
- In senior school classes, some teachers seemed so intent on delivering the information and content that they impeded student learning to the extent that there was little opportunity for students to process information and engage in the more challenging aspects of developing understanding.
- In the majority of classes, the teacher was still doing most of the talking, most of the questioning, and most of the answering of questions. However, in some classrooms teachers were activating students as learning resources for one another. In a number of classrooms, there were discussions with peers, including peer assessment and feedback.
- Most teacher questions were factual or recall questions, and most student questions related to procedure. There was great variation in the extent to which formative assessment processes were in place. In some classrooms, students were unaware of the intended learning or what they needed to demonstrate in order to achieve the intended learning.

After the Visit

To move from formulating patterns to developing next-level-of-work suggestions in the initial phase (2010), after the patterns were developed, they were presented to the whole staff, which broke up into small groups to outline an approach to the next level of work for each pattern, using a specific form (see exhibit 6.2). The commitments each group made to address the individual patterns were then reiterated at the start of the following year.

By 2011, the school used the idea of a theory of action as a way to be more specific about what kind of causal connections it hoped to see as part of the follow-up. It came up with approximately five *if-then* statements, essentially a theory of action for addressing each of the next-level-of-work steps. For example, using the last of the patterns above, related to teacher questioning, the rounds team developed this statement: "If we use meeting time to develop teacher competence in effective questioning, then teachers will be able to utilize higher-order, targeted questions in class, and students will be given the opportunity to engage in higher-order thinking and will more readily be challenged at the appropriate level." It also developed specific follow-up plans (see exhibit 6.3).

As 2011 came to a close, the BBC team crafted an overarching theory of action to drive its improvement work:

> *If all staff are knowledgeable about the links between formative assessment strategies and the facilitation of a growth mindset in our students, and if we all participate in the development of individual and small group action plans for what this will look like in our day-to-day interactions with students, then we will be able to use information from the classroom both effectively to inform our instruction and affectively to help our students and our staff become better learners.*

To achieve this, the team outlined a schoolwide set of approaches:

- We will promote the belief that ability is incremental rather than fixed.
- We will develop and share a common understanding of the five key strategies of formative assessment and provide opportunities for all staff to gain access to this work.
- We will provide feedback that contains a recipe for future action rather than a review of past performance.
- We will develop learning goals with students so they are able to monitor their own progress toward them.

EXHIBIT 6.2

Visit follow-up form, Ballarat Clarendon College

The next level of work	
Pattern to be addressed:	Examples giving rise to the pattern:

What has been done around this pattern in the past?	What are the current initiatives used to address this pattern?	What are the resources available to address this pattern?

Tips:
- Need to be specific and detailed—linked to instructional core
- Go beyond "team study groups" or "use faculty meetings"
- Be wary of broad brush strokes, educational jargon, and indirectness: e.g., Observe each others, share exemplars, do professional development
- Who is doing the work?

Recommendations for moving our learning forward
regarding the pattern being addressed

Short term:	Longer term

Source: Adapted with permission from Jan McClure, Deputy Principal, Ballarat Clarendon College, Victoria, Australia.

EXHIBIT 6.3

Sample follow-up plans tied to pattern on teacher questioning

- **Who:** All staff, facilitated by targeted presenters

- **What:**

  1. Focus of lesson plans, related to Learning Intentions. Develop departmental examples to share and tinker with.

  2. Use Bloom's taxonomy framework to develop tasks to ensure a higher proportion of the tasks would stimulate higher-order thinking.

  3. Develop a bank of higher-order questions.

  4. Definition for analyzing, evaluating, and creating.

- **When:** Departmental Meetings in Term 3.

Re: Next level of work—questioning

- We said we'd like to do some further reading on effective questioning as well as look at some exemplars:
  - A six-page article from Dylan Wiliam on practical techniques for questioning in the classroom
  - A series of question stems that you might use in your classroom
  - Examples of questions that are less effective

- We have all received some reading on effective questioning as well as some exemplars and should be considering the implications for our classrooms. We should also be attempting to refine our own questioning techniques.

- View five-minute snapshot and comment on the teacher questioning.

- Between now and our rounds meeting on the October staff days, please view the videos and make some notes. You may have questions or comments based on your observations that will be worth sharing when we get together.

Source: Adapted with permission from Jan McClure, Deputy Principal, Ballarat Clarendon College, Victoria, Australia.

- We will develop small group and/or individual action plans to work on aspects of the above and will collect information on the effectiveness of these in the next round of instructional rounds observations.

Under this overarching theory of action, individual staff members were then asked to develop their own individual theories of action, based on the evidence collected through rounds. These each included target (*if-then*) statements, action steps, factors to be taken into account, and accountable and success measures for teachers and students.

And then they stopped.

2012: A PAUSE FOR REFLECTION ON IMPACT AND INTENTION

In 2012, BCC took a break from rounds and paused to assess. The team realized that "instructional rounds had become the work rather than supporting the work." While its members saw some initial gains, they did not see the hoped-for impacts in their classrooms and noticed that the initial enthusiasm of the staff was waning. The rounds team looks back on that period:

> Rounds in 2011 was incredibly resource-intensive. It required hours of staff time and significant amounts of administrative support from the facilitators. The results from rounds needed to be significant to justify the effort and commitment required. Some of the measures we used to evaluate the progress of rounds were qualitative. Did student work show signs of the work of the improvement strategy? Were we able to see greater comprehension of the intended learning? Written feedback that is specific and constructive? Class discussions and questioning that allows thinking and reflection?
>
> We also evaluated rounds by observing the behavior of rounds participants during the latter stages of 2011. Rounds works to the degree that it helps people make sense of the multiple demands of existing reform efforts. We felt that if rounds was successful, then we should see signs that participants were more able to see how the improvement efforts were impacting on instruction and, more importantly, student learning in the classroom. This would be apparent by asking staff about their thoughts on what they had seen so far, but also through their willingness to continue the process. What we ended up seeing were signs of disconnect that we were hoping to avoid. Staff needed to be reminded of attending the observation sessions, and there were feelings that rounds was becoming an imposition. These sorts of behaviors showed us that the way in which rounds was being implemented in the school was not sustainable, and perhaps was counterproductive to our efforts to link together the aspects of the improvement efforts.

Furthermore, the team felt weighed down with the demands. "Managing almost a hundred people involved in the program, both logistically and emotionally," was hard. As BCC scaled up rounds, the administration of the process became more and more complex. Those who worked on keeping the process rolling found it increasingly difficult. So they stopped and did a great deal of reflection and learning.

LEARNING FROM TWO YEARS OF SCHOOL-BASED ROUNDS: ASSESSING IMPACTS AND EVOLVING THE PRACTICE

Taking the time to step back from doing rounds, to reflect on what happened, and to think strategically about what next steps should be has led to several powerful lessons learned. Realizing that its efforts were more about "doing rounds" than about the improvements it hoped to get from the practice led the team to do some deep thinking about BCC's theory of action. Making certain assumptions about how adults would learn what was necessary to make changes in their practices in classrooms led to some powerful insights into the school's theories about adult learning. And by stepping back and learning from some of its other, more successful, improvement initiatives, BCC was able to learn some important lessons about follow-up expectations, accountability structures, and roles. Finally, during this pause, Ballarat got clearer about purpose, and had a number of thoughtful reflections about how, during the different phases, it did not always have the same understanding as the staff did about why rounds was being done and how to assess its success.

Theory of Action

Although the team knew from the beginning that rounds was introduced to support the school's improvement strategy, it put most of its energy into making sure that people were learning about the process and protocols and far less into making sure that it had a tight strategy for how rounds was going to help with improvement. Looking back, it now sees BCC's theory of action as far too abstract and too focused on the initial input side (e.g., learning the processes and protocols) with not enough attention paid to the consequent actions (changes in classroom practices and the adult learning that would lead to them) that could ultimately lead to the desired outcomes.

The team had hoped that the rounds practice would help BCC by increasing the frequency of collaboration between staff, particularly across departments, and that greater frequency of observations of practice would lead to more informed discussions of instruction. It also hoped that rounds would help identify the next level of work based on the BCC improvement plan and provide descriptions of any changes in practice as a result of efforts from the improvement agenda. But it was disappointed in achieving these hopes. Although the two years of rounds work led the team to better understand the patterns of teaching and learning at BCC, the experience did not lead to the hoped-for improvements.

To understand better what happened, the rounds team members returned to the theory of action chapter of *Instructional Rounds in Education,* the book that brought them into rounds in the first place—and saw some of the gaps in their own thinking. Deputy principal Jan McClure particularly connected with the idea that "this level of optimism about the direct relationship between a policy and student learning is common, and the people farthest from the daily interactions of the instructional core are most likely to unknowingly subscribe to the 'and then a miracle happens' improvement theory . . . Many systems need a more explicit theory to make their good intentions a reality." This thought left her "wondering why we were not more disturbed by the fact that there was almost no detail about what student progress toward the intended learning would look like anywhere in the planning for learning documents, and certainly no detail of the differing levels of learning that we knew existed in every class. What were we thinking?"

Instructional Rounds in Education suggests the importance of writing a theory of action because it "forces individuals to confront the gaps and holes in their espoused theories and to think hard about exactly what they might mean when they say something . . . The point here is not to develop a definitive theory that is useful once and for all time."[2] But McClure notes that the team spent much more time fine-tuning the expression of the theory than designing and collecting evidence to see if it was having any impacts: "What we discovered, months and years after the 'implementation' of the plan, was that progress was not being tracked as we imagined." She concludes, "The iterations of rounds sat separate from the improvement strategy. Despite warnings that instructional rounds can't compensate for a weak improvement strategy, we implemented it anyway when we were embarking on multiple improvement efforts without a consistent through-line. Although rounds sat alongside and had peripheral relations to the improvement strategy of the school, it was too divorced from the real work, only abstractly adding to, rather than reinforcing, for it to help accelerate other improvement efforts."

Theory of Adult Learning

Another big insight for the team had to do with the assumptions it had made about adult learning. The first was it simply weren't leaving enough time: "We needed a pause in our implementation of rounds in 2012 because we were finding that one phase of rounds was rolling into the next with little time for review and reflection on what had been achieved and how effective the process actually was." The second had to do with the actual model for adult learning—how the team expected staff to learn the new things they needed to do to improve what was going on in their classrooms. The team found this particularly ironic because BCC as a school was heavily investing in using Carol Dweck's work to help it rethink student learning: "One of the realizations we have come to, after a number of recent successes in [other] improvement efforts, is that we need to view adult learning in a very similar light to that of the learning of our students. We [learned we have to] move away from the oft-used 'tell them and they will learn' model (or 'sit n' git') of previous attempts at staff learning, to using smaller teams with a higher degree of transparency to act as the accountability measures."

Follow-Up Expectations, Accountability Structures, and Roles

In retrospect, one of the key things missing in the connection of BCC's rounds work to its improvement efforts was the lack of any clear and binding commitments for follow-up. After a rounds cycle, the whole staff would come together and work in small committees on the next level of work and would summarize next steps on a common form. But there were no clear processes for ensuring that any of the suggestions got implemented, and possibly not even a clearly communicated expectation that they were supposed to be. Reid Smith reflects: "This is the step that was missing from our adult learning strategy in the past; a holdover of an optimistic view that since we were working with professional adults, somehow the same rules didn't apply to their learning as with our own students. The commitments from the next level of work would hardly be called binding, and, despite our rhetoric, our actions would not indicate that there was an expectation that classrooms would operate in a different fashion to how they had in the past."

In 2012, BCC decided to pause to gather its thoughts around how rounds could support its improvement strategy. The rounds team felt that the whole school needed to get a better understanding of what it meant to plan for learning and how to articulate what progress toward the intended learning would look like. Its work on another improvement effort—unrelated to instructional rounds—gave it some ideas that helped address this gap. Working with the planning-for-learning approaches of Grant Wiggins and Jay McTighe, the team used the departmental structure to provide both support and accountability for the various subject teams within the school. At staff meetings, it built in opportunities to share examples and ideas that moved their collective understanding forward. When some of the early-adopter departments embraced the approach and began to share their work at meetings, it created an expectation that every department would contribute to some element of the work. The administrative team constructed a "levels of performance" rubric to accompany the improvement work, and as examples of improved planning for learning emerged, individuals or teams would annotate and share the samples, including insights into the connections they had made. They used public displays of each department's progress. This process created an expectation that all teachers had a responsibility to contribute to the progress of their individual planning and the planning of their team.

Although unconnected to rounds, this work not only put some clear follow-up expectations into place, but helped the team think differently about how to connect some of the dots on the through-line of the theory of action. Another quote from *Instructional Rounds in Education* galvanized its thinking: "If you invest in teacher professional development without a clear understanding of where you expect it to lead in terms of the actual content that students are expected to master, then you get random innovation across classrooms and the innovation has no . . . schoolwide impact on student learning."[3] This led the team to see the need for tighter focus on the "actual content that [staff and students] are expected to master" and to making tighter connections between rounds and improvement efforts.

Finally, the higher level of traction on improvement gained through the Wiggins and McTighe work has resulted in a renewed emphasis on the importance of the heads of department for improvement work, inspiring the team to modify its rounds approach. When rounds started up again, it planned to have most of the observations done by heads of department. Jan McClure explains, "The role of the heads of department in our school is to facilitate the learning of the teachers within their team. When you are responsible for the learning of a group of people, you need to have a strong understanding of what it is you are moving toward, be able to measure the progress of a group, and provide the appropriate feedback scaffolding to help them move forward. Heads of department to be able to fulfill this aspect of their role need to be involved in the observations of the effects of their work, and subsequent modeling and feedback to their team."

Evolving (and Different) Understandings of the Purpose of Rounds

In retrospect, the team acknowledges that it was hard to figure out when and how it should have started evaluating rounds' success in accelerating Ballarat's improvement efforts. In the beginning, it saw significant excitement early in the process. rounds was something new; it allowed staff to think differently about aspects of their practice. This resulted in a number of early gains. There was a greater amount of staff dialogue about instruction, as well as genuine attempts to try to build a common language about what it was that was being observed. The team was patient—too patient, it now realizes. Since it understood rounds to be an ongoing process that would feed into the improvement plan, it was willing to take the time to allow the process to be embedded. It wanted to maintain the momentum that was building with rounds, so it didn't pay attention early enough to whether the process is actually working.

The team hoped that rounds would impact improvement but without a plan in place or even a clear articulation of this purpose, the staff saw rounds as a chance to reduce their isolation and learn from each other. Rounds "quickly became something that people did because they were interested in the process and what it could do for their instruction, and not necessarily because it informed our efforts or helped define what we do. The process itself is so attractive, and we, as a school community, really enjoy the opportunity to see other's classes and discuss what we observed." So initially, the teachers were enthusiastic about what amounted to a very resource-intensive peer observation program, while the members of the planning team were, in their own words "desperately seeking a place for rounds in our improvement plan, since the improvements we saw coming from rounds did not justify the collective resource. For some of the time, rounds was an end in and of itself, which it is never supposed to be."

Not only were they unable to make clear connections between rounds and improvement, but team members report that they were so focused on getting the rounds process right that the whole exercise lost meaning and led to disinvestment of staff: "We often showed too much zeal in picking up statements of judgmentalism. This often meant that fewer statements, free of context, made it through the sharing of observations to the pattern making. Lack of clarity around some of the key terms in the theories of action and the problem of practice, and not being sure about exactly what kinds of things we were looking for meant that many of the observations were not useful. The patterns produced tended towards the vague, and often were pitched at a level that made actually working on them quite difficult to achieve."

This not only led to some staff resistance to the work, but when they got to the more challenging thinking required of the next level of work, they were in trouble. Reid Smith comments: "Broad problems of practice lead to broad next levels of work for which it was difficult for a person or group of people to take responsibility. We found ourselves using the 'then a miracle happens' theory when discussing our next level of work . . . and it didn't change anything. Our failures in this last step undermined the enthusiasm for the process of rounds itself."

One of the big insights during this reflective pause was that the team realized that it hadn't given itself permission to alter the rounds process to meet local circumstances and needs. It had used parts of what it had learned at the Rounds Institute or read in *Instructional Rounds in Education*, focusing strongly on the observations but not doing enough work on the next levels of work and resulting follow-up. As it plans to restart rounds after the hiatus, the team is confident that these adaptations and connections will come in the next step.

PLANS FOR THE FUTURE

A tremendous amount of learning came out of the pause and reflection period, along with a plan that incorporates the team's new insights into the next phase of rounds implementation at BCC. The school plans to go with a model featuring fewer participants, who will be selected on the basis of roles in the school—mostly heads of department and senior staff. The plan is to conduct fewer, more intense rounds—one set per term (perhaps two weeks). The problem of practice will be tied to the current improvement agenda, particularly what students are actually doing in classes to improve their understandings of unit goals and how feedback is given, gathered, and maintained in classes. The planning team's thinking is that this approach to rounds might help it determine where teachers and administrators need extra support in order to improve their practice in classroom in line with the improvement agenda. The thinking behind the shorter cycle for rounds observation is that it would allow time for more follow-up and learning between rounds. The reduced number of participants is a way of scaling back and of stabilizing work that was beginning to become an additional burden on staff. The choice to have heads of department and senior staff as the observers is because they are seen as leading the improvement work and through rounds they could develop a tighter understanding of the common language necessary for the observation.

The team is excited about the future and the opportunities to make much stronger, clearer connections between rounds and improvement. And its members are very honest and reflective about what they have learned about theories of action, about assessing impacts, about adult learning—and most of all about not waiting for a "miracle to happen." Steven Belcher, Head of Curriculum for the Senior School summarizes his learning: "You need to pause between cycles to consolidate what you've learned. Review your theory of action and any problems of practice. It's not necessarily about getting everybody involved in the process. The power is not just in the doing; much of it has to do with the quality of the follow-up." Deputy principal Jan McClure adds: "Every time you pause and reflect on the work, a good place to go is rereading the chapter on the theory of action. Use an iterative loop to take an ever more detailed look at the gaps and contingencies there. What would people need to know to implement that theory of action? And what is your model of adult learning? We have a tendency to apply a different model of learning to adults than we do to students."

PART II

Learning from
School-Based Rounds

CHAPTER 7

Shared Context, Immediacy, and Embeddedness

School-Based Rounds and Improvement

"When the superintendent said his network [the Connecticut Superintendents' Network] would be coming for a visit and he needed a school, I quickly raised my hand for our school. And then I went back to our teachers and said, 'Guess what? We have this wonderful opportunity.' Needless to say, they were not all smiling. But if you have a school that focuses on inquiry, this sounded like something that we should be doing . . . The superintendents came, they observed, made some suggestions, and then they all left. And when it was over, I thought: 'This was very interesting, but we are going to need to make some adaptations . . . '"

—*Marilyn Oat, Principal, Killingly Memorial School*

Instructional rounds, as described in *Instructional Rounds in Education*, is a practice designed to foster improvement and create powerful linkages among the classroom, school, and district levels. In fact, many of the superintendents my colleagues and I work with value participating in rounds because it helps connect them—miles away in their central offices—to what actually takes place in classrooms. It enables them to see how the strategic choices that they make at the district level connect to and shape their schools and the teaching and learning that go on inside them. Visiting classrooms also helps information flow the other way, giving them ideas for school- or district-level policies or practices that can help bring high quality learning to scale in all their classrooms.

Cross-school and cross-district rounds provide those linkages, yet, as Marilyn Oat suggests, they do so on the basis of a relatively short period of time in class-rooms by a group of visitors who are mostly (if not all) outsiders to the school and who leave upon completion of the visit day. School-based rounds, as Oat conceived it, and as it has evolved in the five different contexts discussed in part 1, can pro-vide an approach to instructional improvement that is far more contextualized, intimate, and detailed. Improvements to instructional practice can be both more immediate and more deeply embedded. This chapter uses three lenses—shared context, immediacy, and embeddedness—to identify the potential benefits that school-based rounds might have over cross-site network rounds, as well as the potential downsides of this more intensely local practice. The chapter concludes with suggestions designed to maximize the benefits and minimize the costs.

On school-based rounds, visitors and visited share a tremendous amount of context. When Sharon Hall, one of the rounds facilitators in Akron Public Schools, describes the structure and the amount of time allotted for school visit, she notes that many schools use only half a day for a visit cycle, since most of the first hour of a cross-school visit can be skipped. There is no need to brief outsiders about the structure of the school day, the organization of the students into classes, the com-mon frameworks used by teachers for professional development, the history and development of the problem of practice, among other things.

At the same time, the shared context of a school-based setting offers much more than convenience and time-saving at the setup for the visit. Make a comparison: At a Connecticut Superintendents' Network cross-site visit to Farmington, the observers might get a five- to ten-minute briefing about the Teaching and Learn-ing Framework that drives so much of the instruction in Farmington. They might get another ten minutes on the use of teaming in the district and perhaps some of the other improvement processes that are in place. Another ten or fifteen minutes might be devoted to the problem of practice, where it came from, what the school and/or district has done so far to address it, and where the local educators see themselves as stuck. In the total of thirty to forty-five minutes before they enter classrooms, visitors try to get as much of the background and context as possible. At the end of a visit day, the external visitors will try to integrate what they learned from the problem of practice and the visit to make a set of next-level-of-work sug-gestions that will be useful for the school. In an administrator-only network, that means the visitors will leave a complex set of suggestions with one or two people who will absorb and filter them, and then bring them back to shape the school and the district improvement efforts.[1] By contrast, imagine a teacher on a school-based rounds visit to the same school. She has a deep understanding of the Framework, knows which principle her school has identified as the focus for this year, and what kinds of improvements she's trying to make in her own classroom to address it. She knows what her colleagues have been doing to address it, either as a team or as a school, and where they are stuck. She has what no outsider can get in ten, fifteen, or twenty minutes—the full story of the history and culture of the school, the internal capacity for improvement, the structures put into place for professional development, the use of data by teams, the integration of improvement efforts in a coherent way, and the commitment and sense of efficacy that individuals and teams exhibit. At the end of the day, she knows exactly what type of follow-up to the next-level-of-work suggestions can and will be made; she may even be part of that follow-up.

There are trade-offs for the roles of insiders and outsiders, and they are explored in this chapter. The point is that at each stage in the rounds process—before, during, and after a visit—the shared context, the immediacy, and the embeddedness of school-based rounds provide different options for the way that the steps of the rounds process take place and can be effective in supporting improvement.

SHARED CONTEXT

Shared context creates an intimacy on school-based rounds not generally seen on cross-site visits. It shows up most palpably in the interactions that visitors have with students during their classroom observations. Most visit norms limit contact between visitors and the host teacher during a class visit to a smile, a mouthed "hello" on entrance or "thank you" on exit, so there is no particular way to notice that the visitor may have been teaching alongside the visited teacher for the last decade. But most rounds norms allow, and encourage, visitors to talk to students about their work when it does not cause any disruption in the classroom. During school-based rounds, it becomes apparent that the visiting teachers may not only know the subject and lesson plan intimately (and in Killingly, are likely to have helped develop it at their grade-level team meeting, and be teaching the same lesson the next day), but may have taught the children whose work they are examining.

In contrast to the more generic questions most visitors ask ("What are you doing? Why are you doing it? What kind of feedback will you get on it when it's done?"), in-school visitors will ask more sophisticated, probing questions of kids, like the following examples from a visit on reading in Killingly Memorial School:

- "Why are you doing what you are doing?"
- "Did you make up the questions?"
- "What strategy are you using?"
- "When you are reading, you are trying to figure out that in your head. Talk to me about that. What is your strategy?"
- "What do you do when you don't get it [make sense of the reading]?"

The more intimate knowledge of students and content also shows up after the observations, when visitors are trying to identify patterns and look for evidence that they saw of changes in what the student knows, or of whether students are being pushed outside of their comfort zone, or are able to understand and articulate the concepts behind the work. Since so many rounds visits—in general, cross-site as well as school-based—focus on student thinking, this insider ability to talk and listen to students and to assess their work in much greater detail is a big asset.

The combination of insider contextual knowledge about the school and the intimate knowledge of students and/or content allows school-based rounds to provide much greater detail and depth in focusing on actual classroom practices. At Crouse Community Learning Center in Akron, teachers ask observers for feedback on very specific questions, like what the students in reading groups are doing while the teacher is working with a guided reading group.

IMMEDIACY

Rounds that are held in a common context, where the visit is more detailed in its focus and conducted by close colleagues, as opposed to strangers, can lead to more immediate adjustments in improving practice. In most cross-school or cross-district rounds, the teachers who have been observed do not usually participate in any part of the debrief or next-level-of-work discussions. They typically will have access to the observational data (either at the aggregated level, or usually shared in a way that maximizes the anonymity of the data from any one class or teacher). Most external visitors also leave behind any patterns and next-level-of-work suggestions but typically do not interact with the observed teachers about either. The host principal and any host teachers involved will generally decide when and how to share these data with the rest of the faculty, and the timing of this can vary from a meeting held with faculty at the end of the visit day to a reflection on the data weeks or even months later.

By contrast, in school-based rounds, the sharing of the results and lessons from a rounds visit is generally much more immediate and often more detailed and personal. Teachers who have been observed by their colleagues in Killingly Memorial School get specific feedback on classroom practices before the end of the day. At Garfield High School in Akron, the visiting department will share its findings with the host department before the end of the day. In both contexts, discussions about next steps and what to do about improving instruction in light of the observational findings start immediately. At the Pegasus School of Liberal Arts and Sciences, teachers know that the observations made by the cadre leaders will be incorporated into the next round of the professional development within two weeks. In the Farmington Public Schools, professional learning communities will be discussing findings within days.

Not only can the feedback be much more immediate, so can the changes in practice. The changes can even be driven by the observation itself. A teacher at KMS describes this: "Since I know observers will be asking students what they are doing and why, I make sure all—even the six-year-olds—know what they are working on and why." In Farmington, principal Renee St. Hilaire includes teachers on the pre–problem of practice assessments to get their creative ideas and ownership of the process. But she also knows that ideas generated even at that early stage are likely to show up within days in that teacher's classroom, and quite possibly in the classrooms of the other members of her team.

The follow-up processes after a visit are usually much tighter in school-based rounds. In contrast to some cross-site visits where observations lead to suggestions for large-scale improvements that would require mobilization of multiple teachers and administrators to put into effect, in some of the school-based settings, the next level of work is simply a discussion by the teachers on the team about what commitments they are going to make to try specific approaches to instruction before the next observation cycle. (KMS principal Marilyn Oat describes this problem-solving/brainstorming/planning discussion as "playing in the mud" and thinks of it as the best, most exciting, innovative part of the rounds process.) This immediacy has a number of sources: the use of teams and increased lateral accountability, the more specific focus on classroom practice that shows up in many school-based rounds visits, and the more frequent cycles that are characteristic of some of them. These last two factors are in place at Pegasus, where the mechanisms for improvement come through the work of the cadre leaders on the rounds team in translating what they have observed and learned on their Tuesday rounds visits into the subsequent Wednesday professional development session.

The immediacy of these changes refers to classroom practices but also, in some settings, to policies and the supports for improvement offered at the school or district level. Farmington superintendent Kathleen Greider describes the "ripple effect" of rounds visits and how it can alter the way a school uses its professional development time, coaching visits, and leadership teams. In a small district with tight strategic connections, the learning from a rounds visit can quickly impact district supports and even practices and approaches used in other schools. Akron Public Schools uses data from rounds visits to reflect on the capacity at the school and what kind of improvements need to be made to support it.

EMBEDDEDNESS

Finally, there is an embeddedness to the school-based rounds process that does not—and probably cannot—exist in a cross-site setting. In facilitating or teaching the cross-site rounds practice, my colleagues and I work hard to make sure that rounds is not seen an event—something done once a month—but as part a continuous improvement and learning cycle for the visitors as well as for the visited. We emphasize that what happens before and after is as important, or more important, than what happens on the day of the visit. We stress the need for the development and use of a problem of practice that is rooted in the work of the school and tied to a genuine stuck point in the school's improvement cycle. Without this focus—the development of which needs to start weeks or months before a visit—the rounds may not be meaningful or yield productive information. And we emphasize the importance of consistent follow-up from the learning of the visits—that without those consequent changes in classroom and school (and possibly district) approach to improvement, nothing happens and in fact, the rounds visits can be a de-energizing waste of time.

In school-based rounds, participants do not come together just for the day of the visit; they all live in the before and after. None of them has to speculate about what happened before to lead up to the visit and to the particular problem of practice. None of them leaves after the visit day and wonders what happens. This does not mean all participants in school-based rounds visits have a clear understanding of the local instructional framework, the problem of practice, or why they are doing rounds. None of this is automatic, but the potential for understanding these elements is far greater than in cross-site visits. Similarly, school-based rounds visits do not automatically have clear and consistent follow-ups; in fact, that was probably the most powerful learning for the educators at Ballarat Clarendon College, and the reason the rounds team paused to reset and refocus its practice. But there is certainly a strong potential for it and a sort of "everydayness" to the work as it moves from what in some cross-site settings is, sadly, more of an event—and sometimes even more of a show—to something that focuses on the way insiders work together for improvement. Angela Harper Brooks, principal of Crouse Community Learning Center, captures this: "The more teachers get feedback from the peers, the more likely they are to use it—and the more likely they are to change, because it's their peers who are always there, not those people who were coming in from the outside. You can be somebody different when people from the outsider come in, but you can't be that different person every day in terms of your peers."

CHALLENGES AND CONCERNS

Shared context, immediacy, and local embeddedness have their downsides as well. They trigger questions and concerns about the ways in which school-based instructional rounds is less effective than broader instructional rounds and might even be a practice that undermines the potential of rounds to contribute to instructional and systemic improvement. These may include:

A retreat from deep improvement goals of rounds, which are subverted by teachers who are satisfied with the opportunity to observe each other's practice to share ideas, and in the absence of external visitors, are not likely to work together to achieve fundamental improvement. Individual schools may make rounds an observational approach, disconnected from an improvement strategy rooted in a school (and where appropriate, district) theory of action. There are examples in the cases that document this. One administrator referred to this as the "sexy" aspects of rounds—the opportunity to see, observe, and break down the barriers between teachers in the classrooms—and noted that it made things harder to get teachers involved in the "unsexy" business of engaging in follow-up to the next-level-of-work suggestions. In some settings, teachers were encouraged to "steal ideas," as at Killingly Memorial School, but to not let that become the main purpose of rounds—rather, to consider getting ideas for one's own classroom practice as a part of a larger collective improvement effort. At both Pegasus and Ballarat Clarendon College, early phases of rounds got important boosts from teacher enthusiasm about observing practice; in both settings rounds planners had to make some conscious shifts to help move their staffs beyond seeing rounds as a largely peer observation practice. The experience in these cases certainly raises questions about how many other school-based rounds settings may get stuck here, and not move on to broader improvement.

The possibility that the familiarity of a close, inbred faculty in school-based rounds may make it hard for observers to see problems or challenges in their own collective practice—things that might be apparent to more objective outsiders. Familiarity might also lead to levels of congeniality that prevent teachers who know each well from developing the nonjudgmental descriptive data and analysis that are the key foundations of rounds. Again, there is evidence from the cases that this has been—at least initially—a problem. The rounds coordinator at Pegasus notes that teachers on rounds would want to skip some of the steps of the protocol in their colleagues' classrooms. They struggled sometimes to stick to the facts, especially if they didn't see something during their classroom observation but knew it was on the teacher's lesson plan. A principal in Akron describes the need for periodic external visits to complement the school-based rounds at her school, noting that without outside, more objective, observation, "we might spend too much time patting ourselves on the back."

The isolation of individual schools may preclude any mechanisms for larger scale (e.g., district) improvement. When in-district rounds are working well, each visit provides learning and suggestions for the next level of work for the school being visited as well as for the district. Valuable information about the district's strategy—how it is being implemented (or not), or supported (or not) at the school level—gets transmitted in district rounds. In the stand-alone schools—Pegasus and BCC—important insights were garnered from the rounds visits that have shaped strategies and revised school-level theories of action. But in a larger district setting, do the lessons from school-based rounds get lost? Each of the districts profiled in the case studies has tried to address this challenge in its own way. Farmington Public Schools has set up clear expectations that learnings from rounds may trigger changes in school improvement plans, which would be one of the several ways information might flow up. In this small, tightly connected district, the interlocking nature of vertical rounds, District Leadership Council rounds, a common

Framework for Teaching and Learning and other structures also help. Killingly Public Schools developed a model of nested rounds and has also begun to tap the supervisory structure for principals—working to have principals, for instance, integrate their learning from rounds into the supervisory and planning meetings with the assistant superintendent. For Akron Public Schools, with ten times the number of schools, the challenge of learning from the school-level rounds is bigger—and heightened by the district's decentralized approach to school-based rounds, which encourages diversity and innovation. Akron focuses on school-level improvement capacity, using school self-report as well as the assessments done by the "PACE" team on the school capacity rubric, as a way to track, learn from, and customize support for each school.

CLOSING QUESTIONS

How can school-based rounds take advantage of the deeper instructional improvement gained by shared context, immediacy, and embeddedness without suffering from challenges tied to the relative isolation and potential insularity of the practice? To overcome these challenges, educators involved in school-based rounds need to think about how to answer the following five questions. All five apply to districts; just the last two to stand-alone schools:

1. *How does improvement at the school connect to larger district strategy and learning theory so that individual schools are not engaged in isolated improvement approaches without a larger connection to a coherent strategy?* Put another way, assuming this is desirable, how does information and strategy pass "down" from the central office so that the district remains a coherent "school system" as opposed to a "system of schools?"

2. *How is information passed "up" into the broader system?* Since a key part of district- based or cross-district rounds is identifying implications from a visit for district strategy, learning theory, and support, how is information from school-based rounds shared in ways that also help the district learn and test out its theory of action?

3. *How do schools within the system relate to one another?* In many districts, it is not uncommon for schools to be isolated from each other, sometimes in competitive or judgmental ways (e.g., the staff of two middle schools in town never share instructional improvement approaches with each other,

high school teachers complain about the poor preparation at the middle school, middle school teachers complain about the lack of fundamentals at the elementary school). How can rounds help different schools work with, learn from, and hold one another accountable?

4. *How do schools get healthy inputs from outsiders?* Outsiders will often notice things that insiders take for granted and don't even notice. Because they are not embedded in the context, culture, and traditions of the school, outside visitors may observe and ask questions about things that insiders might simply have missed. Outsiders can also provide access to ideas and approaches that insiders may not know or have thought about. Absent the infusion of outsider ideas teams inside of, the school may work and rework the approaches to a problem without progressing.

5. *How do schools get better at the rounds practice and at using rounds to support instructional improvement?* The subtitle of *Instructional Rounds in Education: A Network Approach to Improving Teaching and Learning* is very deliberate. Networks are key ways to share learning and innovation across different settings. Those involved in school-based rounds who are isolated from others may discover, as Pegasus and Ballarat Clarendon College did, that the practice that they initially developed was not getting them the improvement outcomes for which they had hoped. Each has made some shifts; Pegasus, notably, after interacting at Harvard Graduate School of Education's Rounds Institutes with those engaged in other rounds practices.

Tips and Takeaways

TIPS FOR DISTRICTS

- *Think strategically and then interweave rounds into the strategy.* Every district needs to be addressing questions 1–3, regardless of whether it is involved in district- or school-based rounds. The rounds practice is only one of a number of approaches that school districts will use to implement coherent strategy, inform and shape that strategy by learning from the experience of the school level, and encourage connections between and interdependence of the schools in the system. Entire books have been written on the subject and several of the sites we work with have put them to good use.[2] Our focus here is on how districts use rounds to highlight gaps in their improvement strategies and how they interweave the rounds process with those improvement strategies. Farmington provides examples of both. The district has practices that provide coherence: a common vision for its graduates and a collaboratively developed and widely used Framework for Teaching and Learning, as well as systems practices around the use of teaming, collaborative inquiry, and coaching. These approaches would add to coherence even without an instructional rounds practice, but get a big boost from the way Farmington has woven in District Leadership Council rounds, school-based rounds, and vertical rounds.

- *Develop a nested rounds approach.* Districts seeking to maximize the benefits of school-based rounds and minimize the losses due to isolation will find it helpful to think about how the nested rounds in Killingly Memorial School can provide calibration and outsider ("fresh eyes") input, help individual schools share and improve their school-based practice, and provide vertical as well as lateral (school to school) accountability. Key features of nested rounds include:
  - Frequent cycles of school-based rounds, with visit dates posted well ahead of time. This allows for articulation between the central office and the school, so periodically personnel from central will join a school-based rounds. It will also create opportunities for school-to-school articulation vertically; so periodically visitors from schools who send or receive students participate in rounds. This can be done laterally as well; so, for instance, two or more middle schools in a district send staff to participate in each other's rounds.
  - Network rounds within the district to provide calibration, fresh ideas, and fresh eyes.
  - School-based rounds design sessions, where teachers and administrators engage in separate school-based rounds share their practice and reflect on its impacts and evolution.

See the appendix for a set of reflective tools and planning guide for developing nested rounds.

TIPS FOR STAND-ALONE SCHOOLS

For schools that currently operate in isolation—charter and independent schools that are not part of larger networks—questions 1–3 are moot, but questions 4–5 are quite important. Some suggestions:

- *Form a rounds network.* Find other, comparable schools and form a learning network that will join you for periodic and reciprocal rounds visits. Start with a regional or state association of independent schools, or comparable organizations of charter schools. Charter management organizations also make a great starting point, enabling the affiliated schools to learn from one another about the approaches the organization uses, even as they get the benefits of breaking down the isolation discussed in this chapter. While a network of five or six schools will offer considerably more diversity and input of ideas, even finding one school with which to partner will help open up the doors to outside perspectives ideas and input on teaching practices and to opportunities to reflect on the rounds practice itself, how it has contributed to instructional improvement, and how to continue improving it.

- *Make creative use of outsiders.* In the absence of formal opportunities for a network practice, think creatively and strategically about how to use outsiders to provide insight, accountability, and fresh ideas. Draw on association and network affiliations, alumni, colleges or universities, or other interested stakeholder groups. Figure out ways to change the water in the aquarium.
- *Work to make the familiar strange.* In a large-school setting, take advantage of the relative lack of proximity of different teachers and administrators. Try to include on visit teams—at least periodically—teachers from different departments or grade levels, remembering that this will require overcoming some reluctance that people have to working with those who in fact are further away and less familiar.
- *Build in reviews of your rounds practice.* Ideally with outsiders, but at least with insiders, set up regular opportunities to check in to see if your rounds practices are bringing the desired results and to tune them if they are not. Take the opportunities to go to conferences or institutes where rounds practices are discussed to ensure that you continue to learn.

CHAPTER 8

Making Connections

Tying Together Rounds and Other School Improvement Processes

"You can't talk about rounds without talking about a systems approach to districtwide improvement. Rounds is one of the practices that supports continuous improvement in Farmington. It integrates with others. It ties to teaming, collaborative inquiry, case studies, action research, professional development, and use of data . . . There is a whole system of supports around [addressing an improvement issue]. I would never want anyone to think that rounds and rounds alone would be the one approach to achieve improvement at scale."

—*Kathleen Greider, Superintendent, Farmington Public Schools*

In the last four years, I have stood repeatedly in front of educators from hundreds of schools and districts in ten states and four countries to introduce them to the concepts and practices of instructional rounds. I start each of the workshops with some variations of the same words, reminding the participants, "We are not here to learn about how to *do* instructional rounds. We are here to get better at bringing instructional improvement to scale. Rounds can be an important part of your improvement efforts. Rounds can bring you into classrooms to help you get feedback on how well your improvement strategy is working. Rounds can complement your efforts but cannot replace them."

All the case sites in this book know this. Some have learned it in the last few years. The quotation from Kathleen Greider that opens this chapter captures this understanding and underscores the variety of other systems and practices for improvement that Farmington Public Schools has put into place alongside instructional rounds. This insight was a big *aha* for Akron Public Schools and in the last year and a half has enabled the district to focus on the school-level capacity building needed for schools to use rounds to support their improvement efforts. Ballarat Clarendon College took a pause after two years of conducting repeated cycles of rounds to revisit its strategic improvement theories of action and theories for adult learning to ensure that the adults weren't simply "doing rounds" but were actually getting the learning and improvement they needed from their investment in the process. Pegasus School of Liberal Arts and Sciences got some early gains in opening up classes and sharing teacher practice, but had to revise its strategy and even restructure the organization of its school to get more significant improvements. Killingly Public Schools has launched rounds in each of its schools, but its superintendent still sees significant variability in the learning that each school is getting from the practice.

The issue of how to develop close and complementary connections between instructional rounds and other improvement processes is not unique to school-based rounds. Participants in cross-school or cross-district networks are learning to use each school visit as a way to find out something about the larger systems. Principals and central office personnel in in-district, cross-school settings as well as superintendents in cross-district networks are learning that visits can help them find out if the strategies they have formulated in the central office are visible in classrooms, and if they aren't, how to improve the links between strategy and action. Participants in these networks are learning that if problems of practice are not connected to the real improvement efforts going on at the school (and in the district, if appropriate) then the visits will be sterile and of limited impact. At the end of every school visit, they formulate next-level-of-work suggestions, knowing such suggestions are meaningless unless connected to the existing structures and processes for improvement at the school (and district). These participants have learned the power of rounds to reveal gaps in other improvement processes—sometimes flagging their weakness or absence, and sometimes highlighting their lack of coordinated connection to one another.

While the connection to improvement processes matters for all networks engaged in rounds, there is an immediacy and localness to school-based rounds that puts the issues of connection in much sharper relief. The factors described in chapter 7 show the potential acceleration of the improvement efforts in a school-based setting; and when those improvement processes are not in place, not working, or not connected to one another, school-based rounds will reveal the gaps. As Akron's Ellen McWilliams has learned, "Rounds shines a spotlight on the strengths and weaknesses that you have in your school improvement process as a whole." This chapter uses the connections between school-based rounds and other improvement efforts as a lens to look at ways the schools in these case studies appear to be benefiting from tighter linkages between rounds and five other improvement practices:

- Use of a common instructional framework
- The work of teams and other team improvement efforts
- Professional development
- Administrative observation and monitoring of classrooms
- The school or district's supervision and evaluation system

The chapter explores the potential downside of a blurring of the boundaries between rounds and other practices, and concludes with suggestions for maximizing the benefits and minimizing the risks of overly blurring the boundaries.

AN OVERARCHING INSTRUCTIONAL FRAMEWORK

One of the important benefits of instructional rounds, school-based or cross-site, is the way the practice forces participants to develop common understandings of what good teaching and learning should look like in their setting. There are plenty of schools and school systems in which educators can only talk vaguely about "making sure that we have rigor in all of our classrooms," or "needing to improve student engagement," or "developing higher-order thinking skills." Participants in some of our early rounds networks quickly learned how hard it was to observe and to formulate patterns, predictions, and suggestions for improvement without, for example, a clear, detailed, and common understanding of what network participants meant by "higher-order thinking."

In the last five years, many schools and districts—including several highlighted in the case studies—have developed instructional frameworks to drive their work. Farmington, for example, convened teachers and administrators to support its "Vision of the Farmington Graduate" by developing a clear, detailed, widely understood and accepted Framework for Teaching and Learning. In one way or another, with variable levels of detail and formality, all the other case sites have developed something that says what good teaching and learning should look like in that setting. An instructional framework of any sort will shape the instructional rounds process. The more it is owned and understood by people throughout the school or district, and the more it is used for other purposes like supervision and evaluation or driving other aspects of school improvement, the more likely it is that the instructional framework will interact with the instructional rounds process in some or all of these ways:

- It can shape the formation of a problem of practice, especially if local policy is to focus annually on a particular element of it, as in Farmington.
- It can help develop some commonality of approach among teachers at the school, creating common language on teams as well as connections to ongoing professional development.
- If the framework provides detailed examples of what teachers would be doing, what students would be doing, what tasks would look like in these classrooms, it can be used to provide a much more micro/detailed focus for classroom visits.
- After a visit, particularly if there are repeated observation and improvement cycles, as there are at Pegasus, it can drive micro-level tuning of particular practices, as the example about student and teacher use of academic language at Pegasus illustrates (see chapter 3).

TIGHTER USE OF TEAMS AND STRONGER (AND BLURRIER) CONNECTIONS TO OTHER TEAM IMPROVEMENT EFFORTS

High-quality team functioning and school-based rounds have a symbiotic relationship. Empowered teams with strong norms of lateral accountability can be wonderful venues for every stage of the rounds process—before, during, and after the visit. At the same time, the collective efficacy developed during and after a rounds visit can contribute to development of high-functioning teams. In innovative schools where these connections grow increasingly tight, the boundaries between instructional rounds processes and other team improvement efforts can get increasingly blurry.

For example, as part of the collaborative inquiry process in Farmington, first-grade teachers at East Farms Elementary School prepared a lesson together, took turns teaching it while others observed, tweaked it, and observed it again in a hybrid activity that looked more like lesson study but had some rounds-like qualities to it. In Akron, where individual schools have been encouraged to experiment with customized versions of school-based rounds, teachers have substitute release time and the support of a facilitator/coach for two multiweek improvement cycles each year, which usually includes an instructional rounds cycle. This year at Crouse Community Learning Center, instead of a rounds cycle, teachers opted for something they call a "fishbowl," which is a smaller and more intense version of a visit. The principal, the facilitator/coach for the improvement cycle, and two other teachers come in to observe teachers who were involved with a "100 Book Challenge" on two very specific dimensions: checking on the *just-right* level of the books that students are reading, and specific feedback on the conferencing that the teacher is doing and the notes that he or she is taking during those conferences.

This small team provides immediate feedback directly to the teacher, and the data from the individual visits is then aggregated up to the school level. For example, at the next faculty meeting, the principal will report that in sixteen out of eighteen classes 75 percent of the reading materials were at the *just-right* level or that in fifteen classes, the observers saw that 80 percent of the reading records were properly filled out. The reason the school went from a rounds visit to a fishbowl was, according to the principal, to be more precise and to get a quicker feedback and turnaround cycle. The process uses the instructional rounds funding, has some elements of instructional rounds to it (aggregating up from the classroom data to get a snapshot of practice at the school), but some that are not typical of rounds (giving immediate individual feedback to individual teachers, collecting data on what could be seen as more of an implementation check than an inquiry into practice).

TIGHTER TIES TO INDIVIDUAL AND COLLECTIVE PROFESSIONAL DEVELOPMENT

Since the rounds practice does not generally give feedback to individual teachers, another variation that blurs boundaries is the use of the instructional rounds process for new teachers in Farmington. After using coaching observations, concerns expressed by the new teachers themselves, or other data sources to identify a stuck point for new teachers in a school, those teachers along with their mentors will spend a day observing, patterning, and predicting. Although the findings and suggestions from these visits are shared with the entire faculty, the primary beneficiaries are the new teachers. Rounds in this case becomes a form of customized, individual professional development, followed up as needed with coaching visits, and supervision and evaluation.

At Pegasus, rounds visits have a strong and immediate link with collective professional development. The observations by cadre leaders, made on Tuesdays, are used very specifically to drive and plan professional development on subsequent Wednesdays. Although its practices are not as automatically linked, Farmington also provides multiple examples of how the identification of a stuck point in the observations and insights from observations will be used to shape professional development.

TIGHTER TIES TO OTHER FORMS OF ADMINISTRATIVE MONITORING OF INSTRUCTION

In some of these school-based case sites, rounds is not the only form of classroom observation, beyond the supervisory visits that take place in most schools. In addition to the individual observations for supervisory and evaluative purposes and rounds, some of the schools and systems have put in place other relatively quick observations that are neither evaluative nor part of a rounds structure. Killingly Public Schools uses its calibrated instrument for rigor and relevance in a variety of observational visits. Killingly Memorial School uses its calibrated instrument for rigor and relevance alongside rounds observation, where it serves as a way of tracking an interim measure of improvement. Farmington administrators (sometimes accompanied by one or more teachers) will conduct short (five- to ten-minute) unannounced observations focusing on a particular element of the district's framework. These coaching visits give feedback to the individual teachers and also collect snapshots, using a rubric tied to the particular element of the Framework for Teaching and Learning, that are used to give an aggregate picture of practice at the school on that dimension. These data provide powerful feedback loops, are used to flag issues that may get identified as problems of practice before a visit, and help track any improvements afterward.

TIGHTER CONNECTIONS TO SUPERVISION AND EVALUATION

In environments where there are clear, common understandings of what teacher and student interactions should look like in the presence of content, there may be tighter connections between the work of rounds and the work that administrators do as part of their supervisory and evaluative roles. This stands out clearly at

Pegasus, where the rounds coordinator notes, "What we are looking for in rounds is what they are also trying to look for in the formal observations." Both the rounds problem of practice for the year and the focus for supervision and evaluation for the year are based on the same data and the same theory of what the school needs to improve. Consequently, the observations for these two processes may end up looking quite similar. In fact, if teachers at Pegasus do not improve, say, their work on literacy skills through the rounds observation and professional development cycles, "it will be addressed again in the formal observations."

HOW TIGHT IS TOO TIGHT?

There is a sense of excitement in many of these schools—a sense of gaining traction through improvement cycles and of making strong connections to rounds and other improvement processes and to consequent changes in classroom practices. But as the strong ties between rounds and other processes get built and the distinction between what rounds is and is not gets blurrier, is something lost? The educators in these buildings are rightfully proud to see the gains coming from these practices and pleased to have tight feedback loops that lead to improvement. Does it matter what they are called? Is this blurring of boundaries and labels a problem?

On one level, this blurriness might be a matter of changes in form but not of purpose or philosophy. Farmington conducts rounds-like improvement cycles—with patterns, predictions, and next levels of work—that don't ever have formal visits. Instead, problems of practice are identified from a variety of sources, including student data, administrative coaching visits, and identification by teachers of challenge areas. Regardless of the source, problems are aligned with the district's instructional framework and usually focused on the specific element that the school is addressing in the current year. At an early stage, brief coaching observations may be used to understand the nature of the challenges in the classroom or to verify that it is a widespread problem. In some cases, these coaching observations may lead directly to some sort of adjustment, typically professional development for teachers, which may be followed up by more coaching observations to see if the problem had been addressed—in essence, creating a rounds-like improvement cycle without actual involvement in the process of a rounds visit. In other cases, this process might itself lead to a rounds visit, just as it did at East Farms in the example around math manipulatives (see chapter 5). The integration of rounds processes into other improvement processes can be quite powerful, effective, and organic, even if it blurs the boundaries and possibly changes the structure and flow of improvement around a visit. To keep clear how the different forms of classroom observation—rounds visits, administrative coaching observations, formal and informal supervision and evaluation visits, and collaborative inquiry—are different from one another and mesh with one another, Farmington developed the classroom observation protocols described in chapter 5 (see exhibit 5.2).

At another level, the process can start looking less like instructional rounds and more like an administrative walkthrough. Rounds is usually identified with bottom-up problem-solving based on a locally generated problem of practice with strong norms of collegiality and a focus on improving the systems for instructional improvement as opposed to individually "fixing" teachers. On the other hand, administrative walkthroughs are frequently identified with a top-down checklist of externally determined behaviors that administrators are observing to see if teachers are doing. As Pegasus has tightened its improvement cycles and focused more specifically on a narrower range of instructional practices, has the process edged a little closer to being a walkthrough? Or when Crouse in Akron uses a fishbowl in which teachers are observed by the principal and some colleagues and given specific feedback about the reading level of the just-right books and the extent to which the teacher has been keeping complete reading records (see exhibit 8.1). Or when a principal, departmental leader, and a teacher conduct an administrative coaching visit in Farmington to record evidence related to the particular aspect of the Framework for Teaching and Learning on which the school and/or department is focusing this year? Where does rounds as a collaborative inquiry process end and become more of an implementation check?

These questions get even murkier in any setting that has developed a clear and common agreement about what constitutes high-quality teaching and learning. The boundaries between instructional rounds and walkthroughs get grayer. If teams are focusing intently for the year on a specific aspect of a detailed instructional framework, or are thinking developmentally about moving individuals on a continuum toward a defined practice—and you know what the steps of that practice look like—rounds visits can start looking more like implementation checks. And what happens if teachers are involved in developing the practices that the observers are coming in to see—as have Farmington's teachers and Pegasus's cadre leaders—is the observation still top-down? Is this a walkthrough or has it become a system for supporting collective accountability for improvement?

EXHIBIT 8.1

Tightening the connections at Crouse:
The "fishbowl" and school improvement

These tighter connections are described in this chapter as if they are separate and unconnected. In reality, these closer connections between rounds practice and these other improvement processes often fit together to make for even tighter and more individualized learning loops. The follow-up to the "fishbowl" at Crouse illustrates this. For principal Angela Harper-Brooks, the fishbowls, which will take place across the entire school at approximately the same time, are carefully coordinated attempts to bring about individual and whole-school improvement on an initiative to which the school has committed, the "100 Books Challenge." It is important to her that teachers see the big picture of how their colleagues are doing, and she shares the aggregated data so the teachers and administrators in the school can figure out where they are and where they still need to work, in terms of organizing professional development. But she also shares the individual classroom data at faculty meetings and posts it in public places. She notes, "The more that teachers get feedback from their peers the more likely they are to change their practice. Teachers are just like kids in this way—they want approval from their peers . . . It kind of puts pressure on you to become better." Even though teachers at Crouse may actually observe each other only once or twice a year, Harper Brooks encourages lateral accountability by openly sharing individual classroom data: "So if you are at your [professional learning community] and you see that you have a problem area, that's when you should be reaching out to your colleagues to see 'What can I do to get these scores up or to fix this problem?'"

The public sharing of individual teachers data, she adds, "kind of forces them to reach out to one another." According to the principal, teachers did not immediately embrace the public sharing of their student data and their progress. "There were tears at first, but now the data looks entirely different." She tells a story about a teacher who came to her in tears, and asked her "'What can I do?' She started working much more closely with another teacher and had him coming in to observe her and give her feedback. She has turned things around in her classroom, dramatically increasing the numbers of her students scoring proficient on the state exam."

FOUR QUESTIONS TO ASK TO MAXIMIZE IMPACTS OF SCHOOL-BASED ROUNDS

So what? Does it matter whether we call it *rounds* or *walkthroughs*? It does matter, in my view, if in the blurriness, schools lose some of the important benefits and impacts that rounds can offer. The following four questions will help maximize impacts of school-based rounds.

How Genuine Is the Inquiry into Instructional Practice?

A key question that helps distinguish between rounds and walkthroughs concerns the degree of genuine inquiry and learning that is taking place as part of a rounds process. In a typical walkthrough, the teaching behaviors being observed have been agreed upon before the visit, with observers coming to see if they are being implemented. (Ideally these checklists address all aspects of the instructional core, including what students are doing, what their tasks are, and how that connects to what teachers are doing—but that is not always the case, and many walkthroughs focus mostly on teacher behaviors.) By contrast, rounds looks at classroom practice in a collaborative inquiry mode designed to support norms of professionalized adult learning. Rounds focuses on stuck points—problems of practice—as a way to develop new knowledge and new application of these approaches to the learning of students in the particular setting. So a key question in school-based settings concerns this inquiry-based learning. How much of it is going on? Making the distinction between an implementation check that is more typical of a walkthrough and the collaborative inquiry that characterizes rounds is not to suggest that implementation checks are never good ideas. Rather, the point is that you don't need to ramp up a whole rounds process to check on implementation. Failure to make the distinction could lead to the loss of a key learning opportunity—genuine, ongoing, inquiry into instructional practice—that rounds offers.

How Deep Is the Inquiry?

A closely related question has to do with the depth of inquiry. Does analysis remain at the surface level, responding to symptoms in classrooms without penetrating to deeper root causes? Are educators just throwing quick fixes into classroom improvement? Are there protocols in place like the 5 Whys to help educators focus the inquiry more deeply? For example, consider the opening vignette about literacy strategies at Jefferson Middle School in chapter 1. Visitors were given a list of fourteen strategies that teachers had been trained to use, and then asked to see if students and teachers were using them. One key aspect of the distinction between whether this is primarily an implementation check has to do with the level of inquiry before, during, and after the visit. On one hand, imagine that the school framed this visit by saying: "We saw that we had a problem with literacy attack skills, so we went to a book on literacy development and found the fourteen items on this list. We trained teachers on them and now are asking you to check to see whether they're being used." Compare that to this framing:

We have noticed that our students tend to struggle in our classrooms and on any tests that require them to read a paragraph and answer questions. Last year we conducted a rounds visit where the observers were looking over students' shoulders while they were reading in different subject areas. The observers then asked the students to share their thinking and how they made sense of the content, especially when they got stuck with something unfamiliar. After the visit, the observers analyzed the patterns that they saw and tried to identify root causes. As a follow-up, we researched literacy attack strategies, identified the ones that seemed to make the most sense in our context, and then taught them to the teachers. We already know, from quick supervisory observations and walkthroughs, that in general, the teachers are using the approaches, that they are posted on the walls, and that in some classes they are even taped to the desks. But our metrics on improvement in student literacy skills—test scores and teacher reports—are only slightly better. What we would like you to do when you observe today is to look in fine detail at whether and how the students are using the techniques. Talk to them as they work, see what happens when they are struggling. Help us think about how we can better understand the problem and tune up our approaches so we can get the student skills and learning that we want.

The implementation observations called for in the first example will be helpful for the school, but can be gathered using simpler, less time-consuming approaches. Assembling a group of educators for rounds—whether they are insiders or outsiders to the school—is a more expensive, elaborate process and should be used to provide the depth of learning that is more likely to result from the visit framed in the second example.

Who Is Participating and Learning from Rounds?
Walkthroughs typically provide checks on how well improvement approaches are being implemented and can be used by administrators to modify their approaches to improvement. In that sense, the administrators are doing some individual and organizational learning, the depth of which may vary. In rounds, the inquiry-based deep learning is done by those observing on the rounds visit as they make sense of what they have seen, the patterns they are able to form, and the suggestions for improvement they are able to make. In network and cross-site rounds, relatively few people at the school participate in this learning (being observed in and of itself does not lead to any increased learning). School-based rounds has the potential to dramatically increase the number of teachers at the host school who are active learners in the rounds process. So a third set of questions has to do with:

Who is participating in rounds? Who is learning from it? And how are the results of that learning being used to improve practice?

The answers, not surprisingly, vary across and within the different settings, depending on the different types and forms of rounds being conducted. The math teachers at Garfield High School in Akron initially did not think they had much to learn from the problem of practice the science teachers shared with them, but during the visit noticed patterns that pushed their own thinking about the ways in which they were "rescuing" students and not maintaining cognitive demand.

At Pegasus, the cadre leaders seem to be the big learners in their rounds visits—the ones who build from the observations, patterns, and predictions to design new approaches to teaching. These senior, experienced teachers then share this learning with the larger group of relatively inexperienced teachers at the school during their Wednesday professional development sessions. This model is similar to the next stage of instructional rounds for Ballarat Clarendon College, where the senior staff and heads of department will conduct rounds, learn from them, and then bring that learning back to the departments.

These roles for senior teachers, teacher leaders, and department heads at Pegasus and BCC offer an interesting contrast to the Killingly Memorial School, where all the teachers are engaged in rounds in their grade-level teams. The principal participates with them, mostly to ask questions and to maintain a focus on inquiry and learning for the team. In Farmington as well, all teachers participate as learners in a variety of content-area rounds, vertical rounds, and other forms of collaborative inquiry.

How Does Rounds Help Connect Instructional Improvements in Classrooms with the Larger School (or District) Strategy?

For schools or school districts that strive for strategic, coherent improvement, the enhancement of instruction in a classroom should not be an isolated event. Rather, individual classroom gains should be shaped and supported by system-level policies, practices, and strategic approaches that move down through the system to reach classrooms. Conversely, innovative improvements at the classroom level should move up to provide information that shapes system-level policies and practices. Ideally, the rounds cycle helps strengthen this connection by focusing on all parts of the through-line and providing for a flow of information in each direction.

What happens—what is gained and what is lost—when school-based rounds cycles end up, as most of them do, focusing more on the classroom end of the spectrum? While there's some evidence in Farmington of the results of rounds driving system issues, the trend in school-based rounds seems to be toward localizing and then localizing some more—to the school level, to the department level, and even to the individual level (including the quest for and inclusion of individual and direct feedback). One can argue, as some of the educators involved in these school-based rounds settings would, that the broader cross-site rounds practice focuses too heavily on the other end of the spectrum—on the school and system strategies side. They would argue that teachers who have been observed on a particular visit don't really learn anything from being observed. It is only after the visitors leave that some information gets passed back to them about the patterns and predictions. The next-level-of-work suggestions that are made may take months or years to have an impact.

School-based rounds, on the other hand, tends more toward the local. A rounds facilitator in Akron describes how important it was to add features of local and immediate feedback to gain the buy-in of classroom teachers to the school-based rounds process. "Teachers want something that's personal for each teacher who has been observed," notes rounds facilitator Sharon Hall, "It feeds into the building's problem of practice, but it also satisfies the teacher so that they're willing to participate." Otherwise, in other less personalized models for instructional rounds, she continues, teachers would complain, "You say the same thing every time you come. We could tell you what results you are going to see before you even visit us. We are not getting enough out of this."

Focus on school- or system-based practices does not have to be an either/or choice, but rather an issue of balance between larger school or system issues and more specific classroom-based practices. What is more, it is an issue of connection—How can rounds help make connections between both ends of the spectrum? How does information flow both ways, with the school- or system-level strategy influencing the classroom practice *and* the lessons learned in the classroom influencing the strategy? See exhibit 8.2 for a visual of the through-line between strategy at the school or system level and what happens in classrooms. Note that even without a system, this dynamic applies in stand-alone schools.

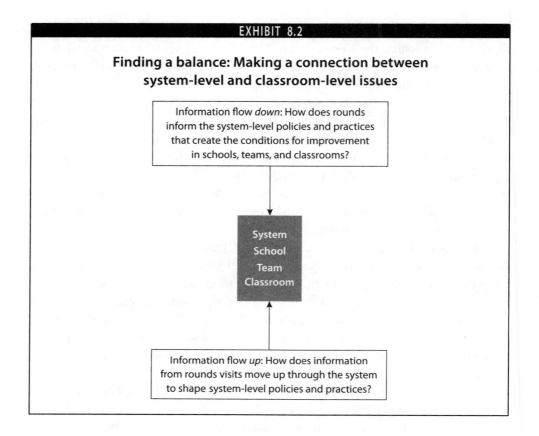

EXHIBIT 8.2

Finding a balance: Making a connection between system-level and classroom-level issues

Information flow *down*: How does rounds inform the system-level policies and practices that create the conditions for improvement in schools, teams, and classrooms?

System
School
Team
Classroom

Information flow *up*: How does information from rounds visits move up through the system to shape system-level policies and practices?

Tips and Takeaways

The point of this discussion about blurring the boundaries between rounds and other improvement practices is less about labeling, or ideological rounds "purity," or making judgments about which practices are good and which are not (e.g., "rounds is good/walk-throughs are bad"). Rather it's about learning. It's about seeing the advantages that rounds can offer through tighter connections with other school improvement processes and also seeing how those practices can be done in ways that may support greater improvement at scale and enhance professional learning for adults. It is a discussion that is provocative not only for tweaking or improving the school-based rounds practice, but for considering how some lessons from school-based rounds might inform the larger cross-site practice; this will be considered further in chapter 10.

School-based rounds offers strong opportunities for educators to connect rounds to five other local improvement processes: use of a common instructional framework, the work of teams and other team improvement efforts, professional development, administrative observation and monitoring of classrooms, and the school or district's supervision and evaluation system. The tight linkages can lead to a potential blurring between the rounds and other approaches, which could result in losing some of the benefits of the rounds practice. To prevent that:

- *Make sure that genuine inquiry into teaching and learning is taking place.* In effective rounds, inquiry goes below the surface and looks at all three parts of the instructional core. This is particularly important if there is a clearly established instructional framework in place that is so specific about classroom practices that rounds visits might become implementation checks. When implementation checks are needed, do them, but do not confuse them with rounds.
- *Think about who is learning from rounds.* Is it the observing team, which is then analyzing, synthesizing, and making recommendation? Are those roles accessible to all or to a subset of the staff? When and how does the learning from a visit get to those who have been visited? What approaches are you using? What implicit and explicit models for adult learning in your setting are you using and how does rounds contribute to them?
- *Integrate and find a balance between school or system issues and local classroom improvement.* Keep in mind that information needs to flow both ways, with the school- or system-level strategy influencing the classroom practice *and* the lessons learned in the classroom influencing the strategy. What mechanisms are in place for that two-way traffic, and how you ensuring an appropriate balance?

CHAPTER 9

Frequency, Professionalism, and Role Change
School-Based Rounds and Cultural Shifts

"If we identify areas that we can work on during the summer, if we can set up rounds with a focused professional development cycle immediately following, if we can involve all staff in the process, then we are going to focus on ways to improve instruction and therefore improve learning for our students."

—Pegasus Charter School's theory of action for instructional improvement

One of the most powerful components of any kind of instructional rounds program—school-based, cross-school, or cross-district—is the opportunity for educators to gather classroom data on a stuck point, make sense of it together, problem-solve, and then plan and implement adjustments that can improve teaching and learning. This cycle—and it is a cycle because after the adjustments are made, the data gathering starts all over again—is the key to the continuous improvement to which each of the case study sites in part 1 aspires. Sometimes called the plan-do-study-act cycle, it shows up in every field when continuous learning is critical, appearing as Lean systems or the Toyota Way (developed by the auto manufacturer but also used in hospitals and medical centers). We know from improvement in other sectors that it helps if the cycle is short and focused, with clear indicators to help track success. We also know that if the improvement is not strictly technical, but requires changes in people's practices and behaviors, the more those people are involved and the more transparent the entire cycle is, the more likely it is that improvement will take place and stick. Moreover, people actively participating in cycles that lead to measurable improvement in their work settings gain a sense of personal and collective efficacy, which can lead to a greater sense of professionalism.[1] The teams or groups they work in develop a greater sense of internal accountability and of responsibility to one another and greater owner-ship of their collective goals, and are more likely to invest in collaborative work with their colleagues and to participate in or suggest other forms of improvement.

Richard Elmore and Michelle Forman, building on the work of internal account-ability and collective efficacy, posit a model that translates these ideas into the educa-tion sector.[2] They argue that leaders create organizational conditions and practices that allow, support, and encourage the efficacy-building improvement loops where teachers, both individually and collectively, are interacting with students in ways that increase that learning and achievement (see exhibit 9.1 for an illustrations of this process). The power of this approach, backed up in a variety of school and dis-trict improvement studies dovetails nicely with instructional rounds.[3]

Rounds puts into place a powerful set of organizational processes that can create the conditions for the Individual and Collective Efficacy Beliefs-Student Achieve-ment loop shown in exhibit 9.1. When done with frequency, rounds creates the opportunities for repeated improvement cycles that contribute to the development of a sense of collective efficacy. When teachers are involved as full professional participants (and not just as those being observed), rounds creates opportunities for ownership, growth in perspective, learning, and overall development. When teachers engage with each other in these new ways, existing relationships with each other and with teacher leaders, department heads, and administrators can change, creating important cultural shifts in professionalizing education.

However, in cross-school and cross-district rounds, issues of scale and fre-quency may make it hard to fully provide these opportunities for professional engagement of teachers, collective efficacy through repeated improvement cycles, and shifts in relationships between teachers, team leaders, department heads, and administrators. Many cross-site rounds are either exclusively for administrators, or only include one, two, or at most a handful of teachers from each school in the process. Typical cross-school networks may only visit a school once, or at most twice, a year; in some settings, visits might be even less frequent. In addition, although these cross-site rounds may develop important learning loops for their networks, because key parts of the improvement process at the school take place before or after the visit day, most of the external visitors are not deeply involved in

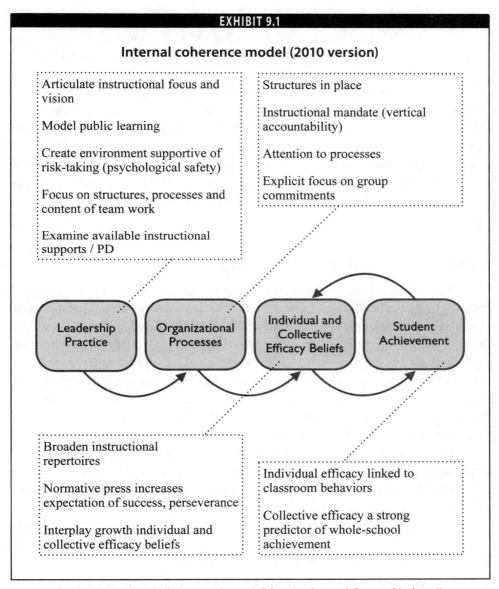

EXHIBIT 9.1

Internal coherence model (2010 version)

Articulate instructional focus and vision

Model public learning

Create environment supportive of risk-taking (psychological safety)

Focus on structures, processes and content of team work

Examine available instructional supports / PD

Structures in place

Instructional mandate (vertical accountability)

Attention to processes

Explicit focus on group commitments

Leadership Practice

Organizational Processes

Individual and Collective Efficacy Beliefs

Student Achievement

Broaden instructional repertoires

Normative press increases expectation of success, perseverance

Interplay growth individual and collective efficacy beliefs

Individual efficacy linked to classroom behaviors

Collective efficacy a strong predictor of whole-school achievement

Source: Richard Elmore and Michelle Forman, Strategic Education Research Partnership, http://ic.serpmedia.org/. Used with permission.

more than a cursory way in the school's improvement cycle. School-based rounds, on the other hand, has the potential to easily address the issues of frequency, the repeated cycle part; scale, the participation of most or even all of the teachers; and completeness, full engagement in the entire improvement cycle.

This chapter takes these related ideas—of setting up repeated, focused, transparent improvement cycles; of professionalizing the role of teachers by involving them with their peers in improvement of the practices that affect their work; and of supporting the ensuing shifts that can emerge in the relationships of teachers, teacher leaders, and administrators—as the final set of lenses with which to look at the data from the five cases in part 1. The chapter outlines the potential benefits, as well as concerns or challenges, ending with ways to minimize the challenges and maximize the benefits where possible.

IMPROVEMENT CYCLES: FREQUENT AND FOCUSED

School-based rounds offers the opportunity for focused repeated improvement cycles. At Pegasus School of Liberal Arts and Sciences, a three-week repeated cycle is a key part of the improvement strategy. At Killingly Memorial School, a seven- or eight-week cycle is used. At both, rounds offers the opportunity to focus on a particular aspect of improving classrooms, use the insights from the observations to spark innovations or additional learning, and then cycle back and observe again. What is important in these settings is not only the improvement itself, but the understanding by the teachers that when they study classroom learning and then make changes in their practice, they are able to get closer to their desired outcomes. It was that ability to help teachers and cadre leaders see their own collective efficacy that excited the leadership team at Pegasus in the opening vignette for chapter 3, not just the fact that there were more examples of academic language used by teachers and students in the classes.

In Farmington Public Schools, the relatively few cycles (typically three per year) for certain types of instructional rounds are supplemented by teacher involvement in a variety of other improvement cycles—collaborative inquiry work or other forms of rounds, like those conducted vertically in the system. In addition, Farmington collects and shares other data, including those from coaching observations, that can provide feedback on issues that have come up in the rounds, which effectively provides other ways to complete an improvement cycle. By using one element of the district's instructional framework to focus on a narrower subset of practice, educators in Farmington are more likely to develop the sense of collective efficacy. Alicia Bowman, principal at West Woods Upper Elementary School, summarizes the benefits: "One of the strengths of having a common focus [by working as a school on one identified element of the Framework] is that we are all heading in the same direction with the same goal. It is more likely that I'll see the follow-up and the follow-through because without a clearly articulated improvement strategy, people feel splintered, unsure about how to focus their efforts."

While Pegasus has had frequent cycles of rounds for years, it has been only since the fall of 2012 that the leadership team decided to stay tight, stay focused, and come back on a subsequent rounds visit to see improvements in one particular instructional area. Virginia Hart, the champion of this approach, had to convince her CEO, Virginia Lannen, to make measurable short-term improvements in service of the longer-term improvements that Lannen wanted to see for the school. She had to convince the cadre leaders to persevere in what felt to them like a bunch of repetitious tasks in the interests of having them develop a sense of collective efficacy.

In Akron Public Schools, limited funding means that there are relatively few cycles—usually one or two a year. While there are some examples of parallel continuous improvement work like those described at Crouse Community Learning Center, Rick Sims at Garfield High School sounds wistful when talking about seeing if the collaboration that came out of last year's math/science visit has made a difference: "I hope to have another rounds cycle soon, and it will be interesting to see if doing this work together will have affected our classroom practice . . . It is all about the funding for substitute money. We have talked about some creative ways about doing it amongst ourselves as a science department and maybe stretch the entire day [of a rounds visit] out over a week—but we all have common planning time, so we are all off at the same time when we could be observing."

Ballarat Clarendon College has realized that it is not enough to build in repetitive cycles. Not only do rounds visits need to be focused on something that matters, but there needs to be learning from the observations, and adjustments to practice before the next round of observations. With too much emphasis on frequency and repetition of observation and not enough on consequent improvement or on using a clear strategy for adult learning, BCC found that repetitive cycles could have a detrimental effect, potentially leading to disinvestment and a lack of a sense of collective efficacy.

In building collective efficacy cycles, it is also worth noting exactly who is participating in them. A full range of teachers participates in rounds—both being observed and observing—in most of the rounds visits in Akron, Killingly, and Farmington. On the other hand, at Pegasus and in the new model planned at BCC, teams of senior teachers, teacher leaders, and heads of department do the observing; the primary role for the majority of teachers is to be observed and then given suggestions for improvement that the more senior teachers and leaders have developed based on their observations and analyses. The comparison across these different school-based settings creates some interesting questions about what the experience of developing collective efficacy is like in these schools and how it might be significantly different for the teacher leaders and heads of department than for the larger group of teachers.

PROFESSIONALIZING TEACHING: FOSTERING INDIVIDUAL AND COLLECTIVE EFFICACY

A few years ago, my rounds colleagues at Harvard Graduate School of Education and I convened facilitators from about ten networks in the United States and Australia to share our practice and to learn from one another. A facilitator from one of the Ohio networks—which had been deliberately conceived of as a vertical network involving teachers, school, central office, and union leaders—was surprised to see so many networks that engaged only principals or superintendents, and blurted out: "Doing instructional rounds without teachers would be like conducting medical rounds without doctors." The comment ruffled a few feathers, particularly among those in the administrator-only networks at the conference, and it has shaped my thinking since. Although I work in, support, and see the reasons for administrator-only networks, my commitment to professionalizing teaching makes me look with considerable interest at the potential that school-based rounds has for a deeper involvement of teachers in the improvement process.

Involvement means not just inclusion in the process—but participating in a different role. The culture change that ideally happens in all rounds—and can happen with an increased number of teachers in school-based rounds—is that the improvement work is not "done to" the teachers but much more done with and by them. This spirit served as a core design principle for Marilyn Oat at Killingly Memorial School as she and her colleagues were inventing a version of school-based rounds there. As noted in chapter 2, she asked, "Instead of looking *at* the teachers, what if we looked *with* the teachers at the students [and what they were learning]?"

The power of engaging frontline personnel like teachers in the improvement work has implications beyond their personal improvement efforts. Rounds can help by providing a collective practice that involves teachers in active roles of interpreting and constructing knowledge and not solely as the recipients of other people's teachings. The individual efficacy stoked by having agency in these improvement cycles can increase teachers' professionalism by providing a practice for learning. And the collective efficacy embedded in the process can transform relationships teachers have with their peers and create different models for professional accountability. This is the underlying goal in the Akron Public Schools' use of rounds—to help "create a culture of examining our professional practice"—and there are multiple examples of it in Akron and in the other settings.

Superintendent Bill Silver of Killingly Public Schools sees this as the core impact of school-based rounds and a key portion of his theory of action for overall district improvement: "The whole thing about school-based rounds is the direct involvement of teachers and the professionalization of the role. That's where I think the whole power of school-based rounds is, as opposed to district or network rounds. It is because teachers are the ones that are observing each other and hopefully are becoming honest with each other, and need to be self reflective enough so they can hear the messages so that they can adjust their instruction accordingly."

It is worth noting that not only is this active learning important for professionalizing teaching, it is essential for teachers to have these experiences if they are to model them for students. Schools that aspire to engage their students through rigor and higher-order thinking skills in their classrooms will not achieve this goal unless teachers are experiencing the opportunity to analyze, synthesize, and then suggest and make improvements in their practice.

This professionalization is, at its core, a collective process. In the school-based settings seen in this book, culture change is taking place at the team level, the school level, and in some places both. Teams, departments, and professional learning communities are natural units for improvement in many of the schools. Their size, relative to that of an entire school, makes it easier to develop a sense of ownership and accountability. The teams are united by having a similar focus—whether it is the third-grade teachers at Killingly Memorial School, the new teachers doing the readers' workshop at West Woods Upper Elementary School in Farmington, or the science department at Garfield High School in Akron. Pegasus has opted for more of a schoolwide improvement cycle, finding the early versions of instructional rounds in departments less effective. BCC, on the other hand, building on a nascent sense of efficacy in other department-related improvement efforts, is heading in the other direction and plans to make departments key parts of the next phase of rounds. Some sites are working to do both. For example, although much of the initial rounds work is done in teams, the Farmington principals bring the patterns and next-level-of-work suggestions to the overall faculty and try to work systematically to ensure schoolwide improvement.

Rounds both benefits from and supports the development of a strong team culture, and in this way can lead to significant changes in professionalization and collective accountability. Richard Elmore and his colleagues note that this is a major shift from traditional models where teachers are responsible only for their own individual students, develop their own individual expectations of students, and respond to vague and loose definitions of accountability.[4] A team that has developed a sense of collective efficacy will see shifts in its members' sense of individual responsibility, the expectations they have for students and their work, and their development of a mutual and collective form of accountability. These influences are bidirectional and mutually reinforcing—the heightened alignment of responsibility, expectations, and accountability contribute to the sense of collective efficacy.

Among the school-based cases in this book, the shift is perhaps the most dramatic at Killingly Memorial School, where the grade-level teams have been the primary structure for the rounds process. Teachers there describe themselves as having moved from the more typical, isolated individual responsibility—"My primary responsibility is to teaching my own class of students"—to a more collective ownership of all the students. Although the school-based rounds practice started with teachers focusing solely on students, the conversations that they had along the way about what was actually taking place in classrooms has pushed them to develop a shared clarity and common language. Teachers have worked hard to develop truly interdependent teams and describe developing trust with one another. "It helped when we focused on students, not on teachers," says one. Another, when asked which came first—trust or the higher level of collegial working on the team—notes, "Rounds helped by making us naked—sharing and exposing our teaching practice led us to trust each other more."

The growing interdependence, the repeated norming of expectations of students through the district's calibrated rigor instrument, and the frequent cycles of developing and then implementing lessons together have changed how teachers think about their own responsibility and what they expect of students. It has also changed to whom they hold themselves accountable. The story that KMS teacher leader Lisa Higgins tells in chapter 2 shows a powerful blend of external accountability—the comments and feedback from "outsiders" in a district rounds visit—and the growing lateral accountability to the other members of the team. Higgins notes that things didn't go as well as they could have the last time there was a district rounds visit because some teachers were "outliers who did what they wanted to do versus what the team had decided to do." But, she adds, "They are coming around; they are saying 'It was clearly evident that I was not giving my kids the same as what you were giving them, and I need to change what I am doing.'" In a related story from the Akron school district, Rick Sims describes how the use of collective, rather than individual, expectations for the science projects agreed on by the science professional learning community raised the rigor level of the assignments and helped keep the teachers from "rescuing" the students by lowering standards.

These shifts represent examples of dramatic changes that can take place in school-based rounds settings. Having a school-based rounds practice does not automatically mean that these culture shifts will take place. While rounds can help support the increased collective efficacy and internal accountability, this will not happen absent a threshold of team functioning and other aspects of structure and culture at the school. Akron found this out the hard way, and it became a powerful lesson in understanding the variability of improvement in its schools and also in figuring out how to best the development of team or professional learning community culture in schools. Farmington very consciously nurtures collective efficacy and accountability with clear support and expectations that show up in its "Teamwork Toolkit" and associated team effectiveness rubrics.

The cases in part 1 represent a diverse group of settings and, not surprisingly, the cultural shifts described here play out differently. For example, in schools like Pegasus, there are big differences in teachers' experience levels. And Pegasus, which has substantial turnover among the newer teachers, has not opted to include all teachers in the observation, analysis, synthesis, and improvement process. Rather, it has chosen to create new roles for a smaller subset of the more senior teachers to do that work. The next section explores how these and other leadership roles are being affected by some of these cultural shifts.

NEW ROLES FOR LEADERS IN SUPPORTING TEACHER COLLECTIVE EFFICACY

When teachers gain a sense of collective efficacy and lateral accountability, the ripples can be quite powerful. Not only does it begin to transform the culture of how they work as teams or possibly as parts of schoolwide faculties, it also can lead to changes in relationship to teacher leaders, department heads, and other administrators. Collective efficacy creates the possibility of shifting away from the culture of compliance that exists in many school settings, where teachers are dependent on administrators to tell them what do. It creates the opportunity for professionalized relationships with engaged, empowered teachers working together with the school leaders for improvement. Figure 9.1 suggests that leadership practice is instrumental in setting up the organizational processes that lead to the individual and collective efficacy beliefs-student achievement loop.

But when the collective efficacy starts to kick in, as it has in some of these school-based settings, what are the implications for the roles of leaders? What leadership practices are best to support and sustain the instructional improvements *and* the cultural shifts among teachers who are now taking more responsibility for their own learning, and for that of their colleagues?

The implications for the choices leaders make about how they approach this aspect of their practice are critical at all levels in the organization. Whether it's the formal authority of the superintendents in the districts or Pegasus's CEO or BCC's head of school, the midlevel authority of the principals or the heads of departments, or the more informal authority of the teacher leaders, the fundamental questions are the same. Assuming the culture shifts from a top-down compliance-oriented system to one characterized by teacher engagement and collective efficacy is desirable, what are the right leadership moves? How do we use our authority to help create engagement and not overuse it and default back to compliance? What is our theory of action for that gradual release of responsibility? And how do we develop the capacity of those closer to the classroom to make informed and engaged choices? What is our theory of learning for that? There is no one "right" answer to these questions of authority, balance, and adult learning. The cases in part 1 do, however, show leaders at all levels in their systems formulating answers and developing their leadership practice to best respond to the opportunities created by these cycles of improvement and the cultural shifts they engender.

For example, all three superintendents at the study sites scaled up school-based instructional rounds in their districts with a mix of authority, expectation, support, and local option. After seeing the successes at Killingly Memorial School, Bill Silver pulled together principals and teachers from all the other schools in the district, gave them support in designing their own versions of rounds, and brought them together periodically to learn from one another and share and improve their practice. He was clear about the overall goal—a customized school-based rounds practice, nested thoughtfully within the district rounds—but was flexible on what that might look like in different settings. In Akron, Ellen McWilliams used district-based rounds as a launching pad to develop the capacity of principals and teachers to design customized versions of rounds for their own school. The district provided facilitator training and assistance for the rounds practice and, more recently, customized support for developing the school improvement processes and practices—instructional leadership, teaming, use of data, etc.—that are the complements to the rounds practice needed for improvement. For Farmington's Kathleen Greider, the growth of school-based rounds was "organic," and she codified the rounds practice in as a way to ensure that everyone had access to it. These superintendents needed to choose how much they wanted rounds to look like their vision versus how much they were willing to genuinely release responsibility and encourage school-level variation. Once they made those decisions, they then needed to figure out how to support the capacity for these school-based rounds practices, and how much and in what ways to keep them coherent so they did not become isolated or fragmented.

It is at the school level that the biggest opportunities exist for cultural changes and for the concomitant shifts in relationship between and among principals, teacher leaders, and teachers. At the school level, principals have had to figure out how to use their authority in ways that support the development and ownership of the process at the teacher, team, and teacher leader level. Some principals choose to be very actively involved in the rounds process. As noted in chapter 2, KMS principal Marilyn Oat would go on every rounds visit, telling her fellow principals, "This *is* my work." She saw her role primarily as the asker of questions and was a strong developer of the teacher leaders involved, but she would always be there. Her superintendent, Bill Silver, respects the importance of developing and empowering teachers in rounds and improvement work and made sure to include teachers and the union president in the initial school-based rounds design workshops. Silver supported Oat's choice to fully participate, although he did not require the other principals in Killingly to do so. While remaining flexible as to how it is structured, Silver notes how important the connection is between the principal and the rounds practice: "The primacy of the role of the principal is really key in school-based rounds. The principal is setting the tone in saying that this is really important. The principal is creating linkages, the first through-lines between the district improvement efforts, the school improvement plans, the data teams, the formative assessments. How does rounds and the problem of practice and the data you generate—how does someone use all that? The principals have got to have their arms wrapped around all those pieces."

Holding on to the big picture of improvement even as they are developing the capacity and encouraging the engagement of the people that report to them is a challenging balance for principals, just as it is for superintendents. They are encouraging—and it some cases shaping—the improvement work done by their teams that comes out of the rounds practice, but they use their authority lightly, releasing responsibility whenever they can. In Akron, even though teacher leaders run the rounds practice, building principals remain involved and remain responsible. The rubrics for school improvement in Akron assess both "Building Leadership (Teachers and Administrators)," as well as "Collaborative Planning Teams," reflecting the mixed and interlinked aspects of development.

In Farmington, West Woods Upper Elementary School principal Alicia Bowman states her goal as "trying to establish a culture of continuous improvement characterized by collective ownership and mutual accountability." Every team in the school has a collaborative goal, which is a part of the evaluation process and connected to the schoolwide focus. Bowman suggests to teachers, "Make a commitment relative to our findings, something that you want to do as a team before next faculty meeting and then come back and tell us about it." She follows up by asking team leaders to bring back their artifacts to share at the next leadership team meeting, or putting teams of teachers on the agenda to discuss progress toward their commitments at the next faculty meeting. Principals in Farmington strategically invite teachers on administrative coaching visits and to engage in other parts of the improvement process, to help develop the capacity and perspective of the teachers, as well as to draw those perspectives into the improvement work of the school.

The same balances of compliance versus engagement, of directing the next step versus developing the capacity of someone else to do it, play out at the team level. For example, the full-time teachers who are designated as team leaders in Killingly Memorial School report the need to learn to have difficult conversations with their colleagues, including how to step back and let other people do the work and make sure not to take it over themselves.

In another setting, in recognition of the importance of helping teachers and leaders use rounds to support improvement work, Pegasus literally restructured itself to create a new midlevel position to facilitate this. Cadre leaders are classroom teachers for four days a week and spend one day a week observing and following up from rounds visits and planning instruction for their colleagues. Unlike the teacher leaders in Killingly, the cadre leaders at Pegasus also have observation and supervisory roles.

At Ballarat Clarendon College, rounds started as a more egalitarian process where teachers and school administrators participated as equals, especially as they were learning the practice. Over time, BCC's leaders felt as if they were not getting traction on improvement with rounds. At the same time, they were having positive experiences with a concurrent improvement effort that used departmental structures and enhanced roles played by heads of department. Consequently, their next step will be to set up a model where the primary rounds observers are senior staff and heads of department—teachers with partial administrative duties—and there is a clear shift and push for them to take more responsibility for leading the improvement efforts in the departments, creating the possibility that they will end up with an approach similar to Pegasus's cadre leaders.

Regardless of the particular choice and leadership configuration taken in these different settings, the common question is the same. How do accountability and authority relationships change when teachers move from compliance roles to be actively engaged in improvement cycles? And the challenge—for any school or district that embraces this as a valuable cultural shift—is how to think differently about authority and adult learning and about vertical and lateral accountability.

In most of our school systems, we tend to over-rely on vertical accountability and compliance to authority. Typically, it is administrators and outside experts who are the source of knowledge about teaching, rather than classroom teachers. Under pressure from external accountability structures, like the use of state test scores, administrators often try to figure out the best ways to teach and then check up through supervision and evaluation (and in some settings, walkthroughs) to see if it is happening. Adult learning in these contexts may look like professional development sessions that are disconnected from classrooms and involve teachers as passive recipients of knowledge. Accountability may look like "getting the test scores up," and organizational learning may be about administrative compliance. Rounds, on the other hand, offers a practice that stands all this on its head. Teachers working in embedded ways in real classrooms are inquiring into student learning and how to improve it. Accountability is not hierarchical or solely in response to external tests. Perhaps the most promising opportunity created by school-based rounds is that of scaling up the internal accountability on teams and the lateral accountability between and among teachers.

To change the culture, it helps to stop thinking of lateral and vertical account-ability as mutually exclusive. The challenge is to develop ways to integrate them: for team leaders to use the right touch with the teachers on the team, for principals to find the right balance of support and expectations with the teams, and so on up the hierarchy. All of this requires all the educators to learn new roles in relation-ship to each other and see these new relationships as opportunities for learning and for overcoming a dysfunctional default culture.

Tips and Takeaways

School-based rounds offers many opportunities to help professionalize teaching and trans-form the relationship among teachers and between teachers and various levels of school administrators. The frequency and focus of school-based rounds create powerful cycles that can promote individual and collective efficacy. The potential of this culture shift is very high, but so is the power of the default culture. It is important to acknowledge this shift and sup-port people in learning their way into these new relationships. Specifically:

- How do you help those in formal and informal leadership roles use their authority to help create engagement and not overuse it in ways that default back to compli-ance? What is your theory of action for that gradual release of responsibility?
- How does each educator develop the capacity of those closer to the classroom to make informed and engaged choices? Specifically, how do superintendents develop the capacity of principals, who develop the capacity of teachers? What is your the-ory of learning for that?
- How do you recognize and use the parallels between superintendents releasing responsibility to principals, principals releasing responsibility to teachers, and teach-ers releasing responsibility to students?

Conclusion

Lessons for School-Based
and Network Rounds

T he school-based rounds practice has tremendous potential for improving teaching and learning at scale and for professionalizing the work of educators. The case studies in the first part of the book offer examples of how school-based rounds can:

- Provide an approach to instructional improvement that is more contextualized, intimate, and detailed than the typical cross-site rounds process; creating more immediate and more deeply embedded improvements to instructional practice
- More tightly connect, at the local level, to other school improvement practices including: use of a common instructional framework, the work of teams and other team improvement efforts, professional development, administrative observation and monitoring of classrooms, and the school or district's supervision and evaluation system
- Engage teachers in frequent, focused instructional improvement cycles that help teachers develop a sense of collective efficacy and involve them in new forms of professionalized accountability relationships with their peers, teacher leaders, department heads, and school administrators

School-based instructional rounds is a variation on the cross-site or network instructional rounds practice. It was not planned or anticipated, but grew out of the adaptations made by many educators. It shows considerable promise in helping to meet the goals of the instructional rounds practice; at the same time, it can blur the boundaries of what rounds is and what it isn't, in ways that might be less effective in reaching those goals. The central argument of this book has been that rounds is not a static program with a rigid set of protocols, but a practice with core guiding principles and key processes that are connected to organizational strategy and theories of learning for individuals, teams and organizations. In the rounds practice we learn the work by doing it, reflecting on it, tuning it, and doing it some more.

Learning from practice and contributing to the organic evolution and improvement of rounds requires three things: *variation*, *selection*, and *replication*. The emerging school-based rounds practice provides plenty of variation. In this book, I have captured several representative examples of this variation and begun the *selection* process—trying to determine whether and how those variations improve the rounds practice. Do these variations actually contribute to instructional and organizational improvement? Are there ways in which the school-based rounds practices could be tweaked that would improve their impacts? Are there lessons from this innovation for the broader network instructional rounds practice? This final chapter provides an opportunity to summarize lessons from and about school-based rounds practices and to share them to make it easier for educator to *replicate* them in ways that may improve school-based instructional rounds, broader network instructional rounds, and the possible connections between them.

My original plan for this concluding chapter had been to develop two closing takeaway lists—one for school-based rounds and one for the broader cross-site instructional rounds practice—emphasizing key points from the lessons learned by examining these cases. But I found that the lists ended up looking quite similar, since both practices aspire to reach the same goals. The differences are not in what each of the practices is trying to do, but in how the unique opportunities of each practice could be tweaked, tuned, or emphasized to take advantage of what that form of the rounds practice has to offer. So what follows is a combined list—lessons for all of us intent on using rounds for instructional and organizational improvement—that focuses on the opportunities that each form of rounds offers, along with suggestions for how they might be more impactful.

The closing suggestions are organized, as they were in chapter 1, around the three qualities of high-functioning schools or systems: clear and common ideas what high-quality teaching and learning should look like, a coherent and strategic approach to systemic improvement, and a collaborative approach to adult learning that is embedded in practice and relies on engagement and inquiry rather than compliance.

CLEAR AND COMMON IDEAS WHAT HIGH-QUALITY TEACHING AND LEARNING SHOULD LOOK LIKE

1. Get Calibrated

Each part of each rounds visit presents opportunities for educators to get clearer and more calibrated around how they think and talk about teaching and learning. Whether it's calibration over broad ideas like *rigor* or *engagement* or fine-tuning expectations for what students will be doing after a mini-lesson in an algebra class, the chance to develop and share deep and precise understandings about teaching and learning is essential for improvement. We can't get better at something if we have different, sloppy, or loose definitions of what it is that we are trying to do. The unchallenged assumptions that we all know what we mean by "higher-order thinking skills" can be a problem in both types of rounds practices. As a facilitator in cross-site rounds, I very explicitly push the outside visitors to make sure they fully understand how their hosts and their fellow visitors are using language about teaching and learning practices. I encourage them not to smile and nod and pretend that they understand something when they don't, since this will undercut a core aspect of the rounds practice. In school-based rounds, educators have considerably more deeply shared context, but that doesn't always prevent loose or sloppy definitions of key ideas. And once imprecise definitions have been used for a while in the school context, it may actually be harder to ask those important calibration questions. While those involved in both sorts of rounds need to pay attention to this reluctance, school-based rounds practitioners need to make sure that familiarity does not breed an unwillingness to question each other. They need to make sure that each rounds visit moves them closer to a clear and common calibration of practice.

2. Go Beyond "Stealing Ideas"

Observing colleagues doing their work is initially one of the most attractive parts of rounds, what one administrator in part 1 called "stealing ideas" and another referred to as the "sexy" part of the practice. Teachers who have long operated in isolation can get excited about seeing others doing what they have been trying to do and getting fresh ideas and approaches. (This is also true for administrators on cross-school rounds.) Exposure to new approaches is particularly attractive at the beginning, as rounds is getting phased in, but becomes problematic if the practice goes no further. Rounds is about school and system improvement and needs to address the full spectrum of issues that connect school and system improvement strategies to what is happening in classrooms. Since there many more efficient, less costly ways of setting up peer observations, it is important to make sure that both school-based and cross-site rounds are not the beginning and the end of the work. This is probably a greater concern in school-based rounds because observers and observed are more likely to be closer in role, and because the focus of the visit is often closer to the classroom end of the spectrum than it is to the school or system strategy end.

3. Stay Curious

Rounds is about inquiry into and continued learning about instructional practice. Ironically, the more successful a school or district has been in developing a set of clear and common ideas about what good teaching and learning look like—one of the principal goals of instructional rounds—the harder it can be to retain an inquiry focus. A well-thought-through and widely adopted instructional framework could become so specific about classroom practices that rounds visits become implementation checks. Such checks can make a lot of sense, especially if a good instructional framework is being used. But, as with peer observation, there are other more efficient, less costly ways of getting that accomplished. Some key aspects of the learning experiences that educators face when they continuously inquire into the core of learning—teachers and students working with each other in the presence of content—get lost if the school or district gets complacent or feels that it has "arrived" once it has published its instructional framework. Implementation checks can (and do) show up as problems in cross-site rounds, but usually for other reasons, since it is much less likely for visitors from different districts to share a common instructional framework. In-district and school-based rounds are more likely to share an instructional framework and consequently have to work harder to remain curious and keep inquiry as a central part of the rounds process.

A COHERENT AND STRATEGIC APPROACH TO SYSTEMIC IMPROVEMENT

4. Get Embedded

In cross-site rounds, every school visit supports the improvement cycle of the rounds network and of the host school (see exhibit 1.1). The visit is a five- or six-hour overlap between two separate groups, each working on its own learning agenda, where few, if any, of the people are in both groups. In an in-district network, the principal and a handful of teachers might be both network members and part of the host team. If it is a superintendents network visit, only one of the visitors—and a distant one at that—has any kind of ongoing connection to the host school improvement cycle. Cross-site networks may (and should) develop strong improvement cycles for the continued learning of their network members, but given the way most are currently configured, they have only a tangential relationship to the host site improvement process. On the other hand, for a school-based rounds practice, there is no need to worry about the learning of an external network. The focus of the learning is solidly on the improvement of the host school. If understanding where a problem of practice has come from, and how the visit represents an opportunity to look deeply at patterns of practice and brainstorm improvements, and then implement them, and then learn from the implementation, then school-based rounds offers something that cross-site rounds does not. School-based rounds is, by definition, embedded.

Cross-site rounds can never approach that level of embeddedness, but it can and should try to come closer. The more network visitors understand and engage with the host school's full cycle of improvement, the more they learn and the more useful the visit is to the hosts and the visitors who are learning how to improve instruction in their own settings. Some cross-site networks try to extend the engagement with the host school before and after the visit. For example, a few years ago, the Connecticut Superintendents' Network started having peer superintendents return to the host school for a mini-visit a few months after the full visit. Those peers now also participate in a pre-visit phone call to discuss the identification of the problem of practice and gain more of the context. Other networks work to more deeply embed the visit into the improvement cycle of the host school by extending the visit day and involving more host school teachers on the visit—to introduce the school, to observe, analyze, and participate actively with outside guests during the next level of work discussions. With more time on the visit day, hosts can provide more context, including information about the improvement structures that are in place, deeper discussions about where the host school is stuck, what has already been tried, and how this particular issue fits into the overall arc of improvement at the school.

5. Support Improvement Capacity

Having a strategy and a theory of action for improvement are necessary but not sufficient. Without having the improvement structures, culture, and processes in place, those theories will just remain theories in the minds of the school and system level leaders who developed them. While rounds does not replace school and system improvement capacity, the practice can highlight the gaps and the weak links in the implementation chain. This is as true for school-based rounds as it is for cross-site rounds; the difference is that because of its localness and intensity of focus, school-based rounds will shed considerably more light on school-based improvement capacity. Like most other aspects of improvement, it helps to view improvement capacity on a developmental continuum, as opposed to an "all or nothing/you either have it or you don't" approach. That allows educators to develop the improvement of capacity in a more nuanced fashion, acknowledging, for instance, that a school may have more developed instructional leadership, and use of data, but needs more work in developing highly functional teacher teams. To guide this work, in some settings educators have developed rubrics to track district and school improvement capacity (see exhibit 4.5 for a sample of Akron's school rubric). Rounds processes—either school-based or cross-site—will not be effective at bringing about improvement absent some minimal threshold in improvement capacity. Doing more rounds, or training people more deeply on rounds, will not solve this problem. Improvement capacity must be built for rounds to work; once rounds is working, the practice will complement and contribute to the improvement capacity development. Educators in both forms of the rounds practice need to attend to this.

6. Go for Balance

If theories of action are the through-lines that connect strategy at the school or system level to what happens in the classroom, which part of the through-line should rounds focus on? What is clear in these cases is that school-based rounds is much more likely to focus on the more local, classroom end of the spectrum, in contrast to cross-site rounds, which more typically focuses on the larger system side. The message here is directed at both types of rounds. School-based practices should not be so relentlessly local that they lose sight of the larger school- or system-level supports, practices, and improvement strategies that need to be in place for large-scale improvement. On the other hand, an exclusively big-picture focus on the part of cross-site rounds can leave teachers frustrated and disconnected, not feeling any benefits from a practice that seems slow-moving and distant. In addition to moving from either/or choices and getting more into balance, both types of rounds practice need to ensure that information flows both ways, with the school- or system-level strategy influencing the classroom practice *and* the lessons learned in the classroom influencing the strategy.

7. Get Nested

While the intimacy, localness, and immediacy of school-based rounds provides many benefits, there is a potential downside of isolation and insularity. *Nested rounds*, where schools participate periodically in rounds with others in the district (or, for stand-alone schools, with other schools with whom they choose to form a network), can provide the outside perspective, outside ideas, and calibration that can help overcome the insularity. But nested rounds works the other way as well. Cross-district rounds (like a superintendent network) or cross-school, in-district rounds will never have the frequency, immediacy, and scale-up potential for involving more teachers, and will not be able to reap the other benefits evidenced in the school-based rounds practices described in this book. Just as school-based rounds practices will benefit from affiliation in the larger nested rounds, it makes total sense for the reverse to be true as well. Some of this seems to naturally occur. The school-based rounds practices in Farmington Public Schools and Killingly Public Schools have their historical roots in the Connecticut Superintendents' Network. Over time, many of the superintendents in that network encouraged the development of in-district, cross-school rounds networks. The school-based versions seem like natural extensions, bringing the practice ever closer to the classroom. I encourage this, and suggest that districts where this is taking place are deliberate about how they structure nested rounds to complement one another and retain the best of both practices.

A COLLABORATIVE APPROACH TO ADULT LEARNING THAT IS EMBEDDED IN PRACTICE AND RELIES ON ENGAGEMENT AND INQUIRY RATHER THAN COMPLIANCE

8. Get Frequent

Rounds visits that take place once or twice a year—or even less frequently in some networks—do not create the momentum for improvement and the concomitant development of collective efficacy described in some of the cases in this book. Infrequent rounds can be isolated and good learning experiences. But without the opportunity to participate in a repeated cycle of observing practice, analyzing patterns, making suggestions that lead to adjustments, and then doing it all over again, educators are unlikely to experience the deep changes in culture and collective accountability. School-based rounds practices have obvious advantages when it comes to frequency. It is impossible to imagine a cross-site rounds practice matching the frequency possible in school-based rounds. Nonetheless, frequency is not automatic in a school-based rounds practice, and school-based settings need to figure out ways to increase their frequency. If lack of substitute money is the biggest obstacle, schools and districts might explore the option devised by Ballarat Clarendon College, where the rounds practice is not completed in one day but stretched out in ways that take advantage of existing preparation and free periods for observations.

9. Scale It Up

The opportunity to engage a variety of teachers as observers, analyzers, and problem solvers, not just as those who have been observed, is one of the biggest benefits that school-based rounds offers. As a simple matter of numbers, it's hard to imagine a cross-site network being able to do that. Many cross-district networks only include administrators (e.g., superintendent networks); the same is true for some in-district (principal-only) networks. Typically, a cross-site, in-district network that does include teachers will have six or seven schools that can offer a maximum of five or six slots per school before the overall numbers per visit start becoming unmanageable. Even with this limitation, it's important for both cross-site and school-based rounds practices to be strategic about who goes on rounds, who learns from rounds, and how the learning from rounds is shared with the teachers who have been observed or with the entire faculty. The cases in this book show some of the options and permutations that exist in school-based rounds settings; for example, all teachers are involved, all teachers are eligible to volunteer to participate, or lead teachers or heads of department conduct the rounds. Given the possibilities for scale in school-based settings, my suggestion is that choices should be tied to strategic approaches to improvement and the school's theory and approach to adult learning. There are far fewer options to increase scale in the cross-site rounds practices. Recently, several of the cross-site rounds networks with which I work have permitted or actively encouraged the participation on the rounds visit of a small number of teachers from the host school. They are not members of the network, but go on the visit in their own school. Typically, these teachers have been involved in the host site's improvement efforts and have been trained in the rounds practices and protocols so they can fully participate in the visit. They can add a significant amount of value by providing additional local context, assuming that clear norms are in place for their openness to outside input and for a lack of defensiveness. These teachers can also be extremely helpful in bringing the patterns and the next-level-of-work suggestions, which they were involved in creating, back to school. Host schools have found these higher levels of involvement helpful in bringing the learning back to the school, in contrast to structures where a principal is the sole conveyor of all the information from the rounds. Even so, this limited local participation, helpful as it is, does not come close to helping cross-site rounds achieve the kinds of scale up that can take place in school-based rounds.

10. Go Deeper, Go Developmental

For rounds to be more than a producer of surface-level solutions to superficial problems, educators need to develop the collaborative learning culture that lets, or even requires, them to dig deeply to understand the root causes of the problems of practice that they face. They need understandings and skills in tackling deep underlying improvement issues. There are technical aspects to this work, like learning a root cause analysis protocol like the 5 Whys, but the real challenges are much more cultural. They require shifting from a *fixed* or *status* mind-set to one that is developmental in nature. They require educators to problem solve in different ways with each other and to hold each other accountable for improvement in ways that go well beyond the default culture of hierarchal compliance. These suggestions apply to both cross-site and school-based rounds, although they may be particularly important for those in school-based settings. On the strategic through-line spectrum between school and system strategy and classroom practices, we have seen that school-based rounds will often focus on the latter. To get the full benefit of the rounds practice, and not make one superficial change after another, educators in school-based settings need to know when and how to go deep.

11. Support Role Changes

Some of the most powerful improvements coming from school-based rounds are the cultural shifts that occur as teachers gain a sense of collective efficacy and work with their peers, team leaders, department heads, and principals in new ways around instructional and organizational improvement. The shifts require new learning on the part of everyone: new expectations of how teachers talk to other teachers and hold them accountable; new ways for those in leadership roles to release responsibility and still make sure that coherent, strategic improvement takes place. Whether their roles involve formal authority (superintendents or school-based leaders) or more informal authority (teacher leaders), all of these leaders will need support in figuring out how they use their authority to help create engagement and not overuse it, so they do not default back to approaches that just require compliance. They need help in figuring out their theories of action for that gradual release of responsibility. They need support as they transition their jobs to increasingly developing the capacity of those closer to the classroom to make informed and engaged choices. They, and the systems that are supporting them, need to think through what their theory of adult learning is and how it has to accommodate and support these cultural shifts. Everyone in these settings needs to figure out what new forms of accountability look like as schools and school systems move from a hierarchical, compliance-based culture to one that focuses on engagement and embedded adult learning. Rounds can accelerate this process, but needs other adult learning supports to sustain it. Although both cross-site and school-based rounds can contribute to this cultural shift, the frequent, focused improvement cycles of school-based rounds that potentially engage many or all teachers can accelerate it and lead to more pressing needs to support the changes.

These suggestions, which apply to both school-based and cross-site rounds practices, are presented as separate items, but in fact they need to be thought about as interwoven and tightly integrated. None of the first three points—about calibration, "stealing ideas," and staying curious—can stand alone. Together they represent a stance, a philosophy, about how adults work with each other to develop, maintain, and continue to learn about common understandings about what high-quality teaching and looks like. The points concerning embedded connection to improvement processes, supporting capacity, balancing classroom issues with school and system strategy, and using nested rounds to get the best of both approaches are all tied together in a strategic approach to improvement and to the role rounds can play in supporting it. Similarly, the opportunities created by more frequent improvement cycles, scaled up to include increasing numbers of teachers, and focused to take deeper, developmental looks at underlying challenges, can help schools move from a hierarchical, compliance driven culture to one where professional educators engage together for instructional and organizational improvement. This is a huge shift, and all the parties involved will need support as they figure out new ways of working with one another and holding each other accountable for the learning of the students in their care. The three overarching ideas about teaching and learning, strategy, and changes in the norms and patterns of how the adults work with one another are like three legs of a stool, each as necessary as the others for the success of the finished product.

None of this is easy, and rounds—drawing on some of the best features of school-based and cross-site practices—can help in this professionalizing process. To do so, the educators participating in rounds need to continue to learn from and evolve the practice. This leads to one last suggestion:

12. Get Smarter

In rounds work, we frequently use the phrase "You learn the work by doing the work." While this is true, just doing the work—without stopping to assess it to see how well it is meeting your goals, without refining it so that it is more impactful, without sharing it with others to learn better ways to approach it—is not good enough. Ballarat Clarendon College learned this the hard way, spending two years of increasingly frustrating experience with rounds before it stopped and then did its most powerful learning.

A key part of the evolutionary story of improvement through rounds is the ability to get smarter as we do it. We get smarter about doing the work by deliberately stopping and reflecting on it. In cross-site rounds, one of the key roles of the network is to periodically pause to take stock of where the network members are and to plan the next steps for network learning. This is an opportunity to look at common problems of practice that have been showing up across sites to see whether there needs to be some additional content or instruction-focused learning for the network. It's also an opportunity to assess the rounds practices that have been put into place, and reflect on what participants have been learning from them—a chance to get smarter about the improvement content as well as get smarter about the rounds work.

In cross-site rounds, the network is a vital venue for the adult learning that takes place through the rounds practice. In school-based rounds, there is no equivalent to the network, and filling the gap—making sure that the educators on these rounds are getting smarter about their content and about their processes—is an important part of the continued learning and continued growth of the school-based rounds practices. While it is sometimes hard to get cross-site networks to stop, reflect, learn, and improve, it appears to be even harder in school-based settings, with no reflective network structure to break through the everydayness, intimacy, and intensity.

This is particularly challenging in stand-alone situations. The school-based case study examples in district settings benefited from their district contexts. There were nested rounds, cross-school visits, and design team meetings in Killingly;

vertical rounds and District Leadership Council rounds in Farmington; and districtwide rounds facilitators in Akron. Working on its own in Australia, Ballarat Clarendon College went through cycle after cycle of rounds before the team acknowledged that it was not getting the impacts it had hoped for. Pegasus was also on its own, although each time the Pegasus team went to a Rounds Institute at the Harvard Graduate School of Education, it took the time to learn from others and to reset its own path for improvement. We get smarter about our practices when we reflect on and share them with others. Schools within districts need to share practice in some form of nested rounds. Isolated school-based rounds practices need to find or set up network opportunities for themselves or figure out ways to get the benefits of the nested rounds that may take place in districts—it's the only way to get better.

The chapter has returned to the core idea of evolution—of rounds as a practice where "we learn the work by doing the work." Rounds continues to evolve by learning and sharing among the those who practice it. Variations are encouraged, and should always be assessed on their ability to positively impact instructional improvement. That has been the spirit and the guiding intent of this book.

In a funny way, although I did not know it then, this book started on the last day of the first Instructional Rounds Institute that we offered at Harvard. It was December 2009, and *Instructional Rounds in Education* had been out for six months. Almost three hundred people from around the world applied for 108 seats in the Institute, mostly from district teams, but we ended up with a few small groups from independent schools, charter schools or stand-alone schools in larger districts with no interest in rounds. At various points during the Institute, they asked me—I'm sure they asked all the faculty—for ideas on how to adapt the rounds practice to their school-based settings. I was polite, I was interested, but I wasn't much help. I remember standing on the last day encouraging the teams from the three schools that had approached me to trade e-mails with each other and to stay in touch. "You'll learn something from each other," I remember saying. "And let me know how it works out." Almost four years later, this is the story of how it worked out. Not just the story of those few schools profiled in this book, but also the hundreds of others that have taken the ideas of rounds—network or cross-site rounds—and created something that is like it, but not exactly the same; something that offers benefits that cross-site rounds cannot and misses some things that cross-site rounds can do quite well. What they have developed doesn't compete with cross-site rounds; school-based and cross-site rounds can and should be complementary.

In thinking about this, I find it helpful to turn to the field of medicine, on which instructional rounds is loosely modeled. Medicine has itself developed a variety of practices—all called *rounds*—and each focused on a particular purpose and audience. The two most familiar forms are patient-centered *daily rounds* in or near hospital rooms where interns, residents, and attending physicians are sharing patient data, diagnosing, and learning together; and *grand rounds* used for teaching, where individual patients are rarely seen and typically an expert is sharing knowledge and practice. Other specialized variations exist, each with its own purpose and theory behind the learning, including *medical case rounds*, or *conference room rounds*, discussing medical decision-making about individual patients who are not present at all; and *multidiscipline rounds* that bring together specialists from different fields to "improve quality and safety of critically ill patients."[1] In medicine, there is clearly a place for variety of rounds; each serves a different purpose, and each can complement the other forms. To me, the same is true in education. The conversation is not about whether one form of rounds is better than another, but about what each of them can do to bring about improvement in our schools. It is about how we continue to learn from and evolve the practice, about how we figure out how they complement each other, and how we nestthem to maximize the learning and contribution of each. And most of all, it's about how we use them as ways to transform the cultures of our schools and create the vibrant school communities that the adults and the students who come to them deserve.

Reflecting On, Improving, and Nesting Instructional Rounds Practice

Two themes that come up over and over in this book are continuously improving rounds in an evolutionary way and valuing the nesting of instructional rounds practices at the school and system or network levels. This appendix provides some practical suggestions for moving forward on both.

The central premise of the book is that rounds is not a rigid program, but a practice with guiding principles and processes that are connected to theories about learning and organizational improvement. For rounds to evolve and grow, it needs to regularly be reflected on, assessed against desired impacts, and tuned. Rounds needs to be periodically and systematically examined to see which practices are more impactful and should be retained and expanded, and which should be weeded out. Rounds needs to be in a state of continuous improvement, to see which combinations of approaches lead to the best outcomes.

The idea of nested rounds grows directly from this reflective, evolutionary approach. Chapters 7, 8, and 9 show the many benefits that their increased frequency and their embeddedness, shared context, and closer connection to local improvement efforts offer. At the same time, they identify how school-based instructional rounds can lose some of the advantages of cross-site or network rounds by being too insular, being excessively focused on classroom improvement issues (to the detriment of system learning), or overly adapting rounds practice so it looks more like implementation checks and loses its vitality and emphasis on inquiry.

Nested rounds take advantage of the benefits of school-based instructional rounds and minimize the downsides. This appendix focuses on how to develop a nested rounds model and at the same time offers some specific reflection tools and processes than can help with continuous improvement. I recommend the appendix to anyone involved with a rounds practice—regardless of whether you are currently involved in school-based, cross-site, or mixed rounds. In a well-constructed nested model, those with cross-site rounds practices will enjoy the benefits of school-based rounds and move their improvement work closer to the classroom. School-based rounds practices that "nest up" will benefit from outside perspective, the influx of fresh ideas, calibration, and the ability to influence and shape the larger environment in which they operate. Even if you already have a nested practice, the approaches suggested here may help you refine it and check that you are getting the most from it. For stand-alone schools without a district with which to nest, I suggest in chapter 7 several ways of finding potential partners with whom to network, to garner some of these benefits. Once partners are found, stand-alone school networks can fairly easily apply some of the key ideas from this appendix to the ways they organize themselves and work together. And all the participants can benefit from weaving some of the reflective approaches into their practice.

Sometimes the nested approaches I advocate in this book just seem to naturally evolve within districts. The case in chapter 5 appears to have been quite organic. Farmington Public Schools is a system with a long history of rounds, strong cultural and collaborative norms, and tight coherence structures (like a common instructional framework). As principals in Farmington saw the benefits of cross-site rounds and began to put internal rounds into place, the district appears to have naturally built in mechanisms to integrate the practices with vertical rounds, content area rounds, and school-based rounds nested within District Leadership Council rounds. The highly organic evolution is unusual, and most districts will need to be more deliberate about developing their nested rounds model.

OVERVIEW OF THE DEVELOPMENT PROCESS FOR SCHOOL-BASED AND NESTED ROUNDS IN KILLINGLY

Killingly Public Schools, described in chapter 2, provides a good example of what thoughtful and planned development of nested rounds might look like. At the beginning, the district had a cross-site district rounds practice and a budding school-based instructional rounds practice in one of its elementary schools, Killingly Memorial School (KMS). Superintendent Bill Silver, seeing the benefits at KMS, wanted to spread the innovation to all the schools in the district. In the fall of 2010, he asked me to help him do this, and to build what we began to call *nested rounds*. His message was an important one in the evolution of rounds practice in the district: every school needed to design and implement a rounds practice, but they did not all have to look like the one at KMS. The schools did need to reflect thoughtfully on their work, share it with one another, and also help the district make the needed adjustments to the district rounds to maximize the local and district learning.

In creating this appendix, I have used the experience of working with Killingly as an opportunity to lay out some tools and processes to be used developmentally over time. It is a story about building a nested practice, but it is also a story about continuous improvement, scaling up, and evolving to better meet improvement goals. I have focused in what follows more on the approaches and instruments we used than on the responses from Killingly, or exactly what decisions it used in scaling up its school-based practices and creating a nested one. Those details—how it revamped the purposes and frequency of district rounds, how it arranged schedules to maximize crossover between schools and outsider input into schools—are outlined in chapter 2. Here, I use the district's story and its developmental timeline and process to suggest some ways for readers to refine and improve their own practices and to develop a customized version of nested rounds for their own setting.

Phase 1—Developing School-Based and District Rounds Practices

Chapter 2 describes the situation in the fall of 2010 when Silver convened a design team comprising administrators and teachers from each school to ramp up school-based rounds and adjust network rounds. In this sense, the period described in the opening of the chapter (2008–2010) can be considered Phase 1 of rounds development in Killingly. Building from Silver's experience in the Connecticut Superintendents' Network, there was a nascent school-based practice in one school (and some discussions of starting one in another) and semiannual district visits to each school. Until 2010, each school operated relatively autonomously, although there were some unifying practices (e.g., rounds itself, the district's focus on rigor and on literacy). Silver saw missed opportunities and was determined to learn from the separate practices and evolve to something that was impactful, districtwide, and coherent.

Phase 2—Learning from One School, Designing Customized Versions for All Schools, Beginning Nesting

Superintendent Silver's approach mirrored the evolutionary development metaphor that is woven into this book. An innovative practice that already was showing some benefits had been developed in one of the schools, and Silver wanted educators in the other schools to learn from the KMS model and to develop innovations of their own. To ensure a broad ownership and involvement in this rounds improvement effort, Silver made sure that the schools' individual design teams included teachers as well as administrators, and that the union president was involved from the outset. This reflective and evolutionary philosophy drove the agenda for the first two-day observation and design workshop in December 2010 and the framing of the goals for those sessions:

- Build on current school-based rounds, including making sure they are connected to other instructional improvement efforts (e.g., data teams)
- Scale up school-based rounds so a locally customized version is being developed for all schools and tied to school and district instructional improvement efforts
- Tie back to the purposes and steps of network-based rounds—how the network or cross-site rounds is usually done—to calibrate and work on hard parts
- Determine how the district can best support school-based rounds:
  □ Share practices across schools; support schools in developing
  □ Coordinate school-based rounds with district-level rounds
  □ Ensure school-based rounds is part of a larger, coherent instructional improvement strategy

The agenda for the first day (see exhibit A.1) provided all the participants with a chance to calibrate on the broader goals and practices of (network-based) rounds. This was done through readings and a presentation/discussion with me and provided important context for the main event of the day, which was to be participant/observers on a school-based rounds visit in Killingly Memorial School. The non-KMS people observed in classrooms, but were then silent observers of a "fishbowl" as the KMS staff conducted their normal debriefing.

At a few points during the fishbowl, the guests had the chance to ask questions (to "punctuate" the fishbowl), but questions were mostly saved until the end. The guests used the "Meta Observation Sheet" (see exhibit A.2) to keep track of their

EXHIBIT A.1	
Day 1 agenda	
8:00	Welcome and Introduction • Warm-up about rounds • What is rounds and how does it tie to your work? • Practicing the muscle of seeing
8:45	Introduction to today's rounds
9:00	Observations
10:00	Debrief observation in a punctuated fishbowl
11:30	Feedback (and questions) on the debriefing
12:00	Lunch
1:00	Evolution of building-level rounds process
2:00	Summary of the day and planning for Friday
3:00	Closure: Reflecting on our learning

questions and to take notes on ideas they might want to use for their own school design. After the principal and teachers at KMS described the evolution of their school-based rounds model, guests had a chance to think about the implications for their own school design and also about what district rounds should look like to best integrate and support the school-based models.

The second day (see exhibit A.3) gave the participants design time and space—opportunities to work as teams on their customized plans, and to share them with educators from one or two other schools. This not only gave them the opportunity to get feedback through a tuning protocol, but it also let the educators from the different schools take an early look at what their colleagues were planning.

Exhibit A.4 shows the planning sheet used by each school. In order to take a serious look at how to improve in-district cross-school rounds, it made sense for this mixed group of teachers and administrators to develop an honest assessment of what was working well and what was not in the way the district went about the business of instructional and organizational improvement. Any suggestions

Meta observation sheet

All rounds processes are parts of improvement cycles. There is always work before and after the actual rounds visit, although visitors have to ask about it, since they won't see it. Use this note-taker to jot down what you are noticing about the rounds process that we are observing (not about the classes we are visiting). We will use this to stimulate questions for the principal and school leadership team and for our debrief.

	Prior work	Observation	Debriefing	Follow-up work
What do you notice about each segment that seems like it contributes to the school's instructional improvement work?				
What clarifying questions do you have about each segment? (Clarifying questions are matters of fact with generally short answers.)				
What probing questions do you have—things you are wondering about? (These might get to some of the underlying philosophy or design choices made at the school; also might include stretches or improvements.)				
What are you wondering about in terms of bringing any of these ideas back to your own school?				
When you think about each school doing school-based rounds, what are some of the implications or questions for the *district*?				

	EXHIBIT A.3

Day 2 agenda

8:00	Instructional improvement districtwide
	• What is working and what is not?
	• How does rounds fit in?
8:40	Revisit larger framing of rounds improvement cycle
	• Problem of practice development
	• Ties to improvement cycle
	• Questions from day 1 (break included)
10: 30	Action planning for each school and district team
1:00	Split group visit and feedback—tuning protocol
2:00	Reconvene
	• Each school's commitments
	• Design criteria for district rounds and support
3:00	Closure: Reflecting on our learning

for refinements of the in-district rounds, or proposals for nesting of the rounds, needed to be grounded in this honest assessment. The second day ended with commitments, with each school outlining the work that it would be doing over the next six months.

Phase 3—Learning from the Startups in All the Schools, Checking for Impacts, and Tuning the Process

Between December 2010 and May 2011, each of the Killingly schools put its customized plan for school-based rounds into practice. The same design team of teachers and administrators met for two days in May at the high school. The first day was also a rounds visit day, with the team observing in classrooms and looking over the shoulders of the high school teachers and administrators as they conducted what they had developed as their school-based rounds process. Participants used the same Meta Observation Sheet (exhibit A.2) to track their observations, questions, and insights. The goals, however were different, reflective of

---

EXHIBIT A.4

Action plan for your school-based rounds

Guidelines:

- They don't all have to look the same.
- They do all have to tie to your school's improvement processes.
- They should all take advantage of S←—→S and S←—→D connections
- They should be clear, actionable, with your next steps outlined.

Design questions:

Describe the school based rounds model you have in mind to implement.

The rounds model

- Who is in it? How is it organized (grade level, department, etc.?)
- How often and when do the participants meet? Voluntary? Mandatory?
- How will you manage the logistics (coverage, etc.)

Learning from rounds

- What will happen before and after the visits to tune the rounds and to support improvement? How will you select problems of practice? Follow up?
- Aside from visits, what are the other ways that the participants will learn together? How will you bring in outside innovative ideas?
- What connections will rounds have to your school improvement processes?
- How will you calibrate your rounds groups (both inside your school and with others in your district)?

Connections

- What will connect your school-based rounds to those in other district schools and to the district's improvement efforts?
- Who will facilitate and what is the role of the facilitator in keeping the connection between rounds and system/school improvement processes?
- What suggestions do you have for how the district can support your school-based rounds—through the design of district-based rounds or otherwise?

For Friday:

Think about what you can commit to for happens next:
(By Monday, by the end of January, by June)

Questions to consider:

• What will happen to this planning group?

• What obstacles, challenges do you expect?

• What is the process for getting from the group to others in your school?

• What is the process for familiarization others with rounds?

• How will you model the process?

WHO IS COMMITTING TO WHAT, AND BY WHEN?
WHO IS ACCOUNTABLE TO WHOM, AND FOR WHAT?

the fact that all of the schools had had a chance to develop a rounds practice and could now be more sophisticated in learning from each other's practices in making connections between rounds approaches and instructional improvement. During the day, for example, after observing the high school's practices, the participants were invited to discuss what they had noticed about connections between Killingly High School's rounds and improvement—not only what they noticed at the high school, but what connections it had for the work in their own school, and what questions and implications it raised for district rounds. The next day was a sharing, consolidation, and tuning day. It started with each school sharing a one-minute description of its model's logistics—who visits whom, when, etc.—followed by three ideas that it had tried that were working and that it wanted to share with others. In addition, each school team shared two questions—things the school was struggling with, or were not working as well as had been hoped. Each of these mini-presentations ended with a connection that each school had made between its school-based rounds process and school improvement.

In the evolutionary spirit of "innovate, assess and share impacts, and replicate," educators from each of the schools reorganized into four groups to try to identify what "good practice" would look like for each of the four phases of school-based rounds identified on their Meta Observation Sheet. "Good practice" was defined as what works to lead to instructional improvement. Teams were asked to draw on what they had seen the day before at the high school as well as what they were learning was impactful in their own practice, focusing on the following four categories:

- *Prior work:* Including problem of practice development, prep, involvement plus ownership of teachers and connections to school improvement plans
- *Observation:* How structured, by whom; kinds and focus of descriptive data; focus on students, teachers, task
- *Debriefing:* Including. who talks to whom and what they talk about—patternmaking, prediction, recommendations for what's next
- *Follow-up work:* Who follows up with whom—vertical and lateral accountability; ties to school as well as district improvement work

The school teams then had the opportunity to integrate what they were seeing and learning as part of their own local continuous improvement of the rounds efforts. Drawing on the notes they taken the day before, the ideas that they had heard from other schools, their own identification of things that were not yet working well in their own practice, and the good practices that they and their colleagues had identified, the individual teams identified next steps for improvement that they wished to implement in the coming school year. They were asked to identify the improvements they wanted to try, specify who would do them and how they would be implemented, and outline specifically how they would check to see if these innovations were resulting in improved instruction. Later in the day, they shared their ideas and received a brief round of feedback from other teams (see exhibit A.5).

EXHIBIT A.5

Step-back consultancy protocol

3 minutes	Presenting school: Explain your plan
2 minutes	Consultants: Ask clarifying questions
5 minutes	Presenters: Step back and silently listen as consultants have a discussion in which they provide warm feedback, cool feedback, and a stretch (an idea that might stretch their thinking, that is relevant but they might not have thought about yet)
2 minutes	Presenters: Step in and all talk together

Meanwhile, the central office staff met to discuss some of the suggestions that participants had made for how district rounds could be improved. At the end of the day, the entire group discussed what district rounds should look like to support school-based instructional rounds and instructional improvement, specifically around providing calibration of the rounds practice and districtwide improvement practices and sources of outside ideas/perspective. In addition, they discussed how a nested rounds practice could support system learning as well as school-to-school learning, could foster lateral as well as vertical accountability, and overall contribute to coherent improvement in the district.

Phase 4—Continuous Improvement and Refining the Practice

Halfway into the next school year, the design team reconvened for a one-day session, which focused less on the logistics of the school-based and district-based rounds models and more on the consequent learning from and the connections between them. In preparation for this session in February 2012, school teams were asked prepare a reflective practice worksheet (see exhibit A.6) and to meet ahead of time and respond to questions about what they were actually doing in their school-based rounds, what was working well, and what data sources they were using to assess their progress. Teams were asked to bring their questions and "stuck" points to the session, and to think ahead to ways the district (through district-based rounds and otherwise) could help support the work in their school.

Teams were asked to bring artifacts from two of their rounds visits over the last several months—one they considered effective in improving instruction, and one they thought was less effective. Artifacts included:

- Problems of practice, any condensed notes from the visit, including the next level of work (or whatever action-oriented equivalent set of recommendations they had from the visit), and their notes on what actually happened afterward as a result of the visit
- Any data (test scores, changes in teacher practices, changes on level of rigor, etc.) that the school has been using to track improvements

The artifacts were a key element of this session. Because all the schools had a year or more of rounds practice, there was a real opportunity to draw on that to do some collective learning. Participants were asked to conduct an artifact analysis and scouting protocol (see exhibit A.7) that they used to begin reflecting—in their school teams—on the artifacts.

	EXHIBIT A.6	

Reflective practice worksheet

Design questions:

Describe the school based rounds model you set up in your school

The rounds model

- Who is in it? How is it organized (grade level, department, etc.?)
- How often and when do the participants meet? Voluntary? Mandatory?
- How are you managing the logistics (coverage, etc.)

What did you actually do?	*What is working?* *How do you know?*	*Questions, stuck points?*

Learning from rounds

- What happens before and after the visits to tune the rounds and to support improvement? How do you select problems of practice? Follow up?
- What happens after the visits with the data collected?
- Aside from visits, what are the other ways that the participants learn together? How do you bring in outside innovative ideas?
- What connections does rounds have to your school improvement processes?
- How do you calibrate your rounds groups (both inside your school and with others in your district)?

What did you actually do?	*What is working?* *How do you know?*	*Questions, stuck points?*

Connections

- What connects your school-based rounds to those in other district schools and to the district's improvement efforts?

- Who facilitates and what is the role of the facilitator in keeping the connection between rounds and system/school improvement processes?
- What suggestions do you have for how the district can support your school-based rounds—through the design of district-based rounds or otherwise?

What did you actually do?	What is working? How do you know?	Questions, stuck points?

Since the way to improve rounds is to connect it to the outcomes of instructional improvement, the protocol encouraged teams to pay attention to the evidence they were using to determine which visits cycles were more successful than others. In the "scouting" portion of the protocol, participants needed to find two people from two other schools to share and discuss their insights with. After this opportunity

---

EXHIBIT A.7

Artifact analysis and scouting protocol

Step 1: As a school, analyze the artifacts you brought from a more and a less successful rounds visit cycle. Discuss:

- What visits seemed to result in the most powerful connection between rounds and instructional improvement or other learning?
- How do you know? What evidence would you cite?
- What visits seemed to have less successful connections between rounds and instructional improvement or other learning?
- How do you know? What evidence would you cite?
- What factors led to that success? What led to the weaker visit cycles? What can you learn from these differences that can shape your continuing design improvements?

Step 2: Find two people from two other schools and share your answers to these questions.

Step 3: Return to your school and share what you heard from other schools.

Step 4: Consolidate and refine plans for coming year.

to learn the lessons as well as the innovations from other schools, teams returned to consolidate and refine their plans for the coming year. Once again the session concluded by focusing on the nested portion of the work—reflecting on the changes that had been put into place following the discussion the previous May, and making plans for additional refinements, moving forward.

Tips and Takeaways

The refinement and development of a nested rounds practice cannot be done in a one-size-fits-all fashion, but must be customized to the context and needs of a particular setting. This is true whether you are looking at school-based rounds in a district context or in a stand-alone school setting. In this appendix, I have focused on the questions and the organizational processes that were used to help Killingly Public Schools develop its nested practice, rather than on the particular model it developed. I invite readers to adapt this iterative reflective practice, along with the questions, activities, and prompts embedded in it into their own settings. A few closing thoughts and suggestions:

- Think about both the process and the product that you hope to achieve through nested rounds—not only what nested rounds might look like, but what kinds of collaborative and culture-building processes you wish to build in.
- Be creative in fostering innovation and figuring out how to share it—across the schools in a district or in a network of stand-alone schools, or even across departments or teams within a large school:
  □ Start some variation in practice.
  □ Agree on some interim measures to help identify desirable impacts.
  □ Based on that process, identify some elements of "good practice."
  □ Figure out how to share innovations as well as approaches to assessment across sites.
  □ Let that process drive improvement.

Avoid the pitfalls of fragmentation by harnessing the individual innovations and improvements into a nested system that encourages calibration, outside perspective and ideas, vertical as well as lateral accountability, and overall coherence and system learning.

Manage the entire process with just the right amount of authority and structure—enough to foster innovation and set up clear expectations, but not so much that participants get stuck in the compliance mode, rather than develop ownership of the process and the outcomes.

Finally, develop the habit of reflection and of examination of how well rounds is contributing to improvement, so you and your colleagues are less likely to just "do" rounds, but will keep your eyes on the real prize—continuous organizational and instructional improvement at scale.

NOTES

Introduction

1. Elizabeth A. City, Richard F. Elmore, Sarah E. Fiarman, and Lee Teitel, *Instructional Rounds in Education* (Cambridge, MA: Harvard Education Press, 2009).
2. David Tyack and Larry Cuban, *Tinkering Toward Utopia: A Century of Public School Reform* (Cambridge, MA: Harvard University Press, 1995).

Chapter 1

1. The first part of this chapter is an update and modification of Lee Teitel, "Improving Teaching and Learning Through Instructional Rounds," *Harvard Educational Letter* May/June 2009. The opening vignette is an illustrative scenario, drawn from a combination of experiences of instructional rounds visits and originally shared in the work just cited. The second and third parts are adaptations and updates from Elizabeth A. City, Richard F. Elmore, Sarah E. Fiarman, and Lee Teitel, *Instructional Rounds in Education* (Cambridge, MA: Harvard Education Press, 2009), especially, but not entirely, from chapters 8 and 9 and the epilogue.
2. City et al., *Instructional Rounds in Education*, 185.
3. Rachel E. Curtis and Elizabeth A. City, *Strategy in Action: How School Systems Can Support Powerful Learning and Teaching* (Cambridge, MA: Harvard Education Press, 2009); Kathryn P. Boudett, Elizabeth A. City, Richard J. Murnane, eds., *Data Wise: A Step-by-Step Guide to Using Assessment Results to Improve Teaching And Learning* (Cambridge, MA: Harvard Education Press, 2005).
4. Philosophically, the developmental approach draws on the work of Carol Dweck, *Mindset: The New Psychology of Success* (New York: Random House, 2006). Victoria, Australia, uses a developmental approach for student and teacher learning as well as for organizational development. For example of this approach applied to school leaders, see https://www.eduweb.vic.gov.au/edulibrary/public/staffdev/bastowinstitute/DLFposter.pdf.

Chapter 3

1. Project Zero and Reggio Children, *Making Learning Visible: Children as Individual and Group Learners* (Reggio Emilia, Italy: Reggio Children, 2001).

Chapter 5

1. Pseudonyms have been used for the students in this vignette.

Chapter 6

1. In addition to interviews over Skype, much of my communication with the Australian team has been through email and writing. In many cases they chose to write collective responses

to my queries. For much of this chapter, I am using their responses to questions with slight adaptations or paraphrasing. The text delineated by quotation marks represents their collective written response, so it is attributed to "the team," or "the school." Comments made in separate e-mails or in interviews that are attributable to an identified individual are so designated.

2. Elizabeth A. City, Richard F. Elmore, Sarah E. Fiarman, and Lee Teitel, *Instructional Rounds in Education* (Cambridge, MA: Harvard Education Press, 2009), 43.

3. Ibid., 25.

Chapter 7

1. Some administrator networks, including the Connecticut Superintendents' Network, encourage the host districts to include up to a set number (often five or six) teachers as part of the visit team. This changes the dynamic somewhat, and allows other people besides the principal to bring the data, findings, and interpretations back to the staff. It is still different on these factors from school-based rounds, but not as dramatically so.

2. For example, some use Rachel Curtis and Elizabeth City, *Strategy in Action: How School Systems Can Support Powerful Learning and Teaching* (Cambridge, MA: Harvard Education Press, 2009) or the case-based approach of Stacy Childress, Richard F. Elmore, Allen Grossman, and Susan Moore Johnson, *Managing School Districts for High Performance* (Cambridge, MA: Harvard Education Press, 2007).

Chapter 9

1. Atul Gawande, *Better* (New York: Picador, 2007).

2. Richard Elmore and Michelle Forman, Strategic Education Research Partnership, http://ic.serpmedia.org/.

3. For improvement studies, see, for instance, Anthony S. Bryk et al., *Organizing Schools for Improvement: Lessons from Chicago* (University of Chicago Press, 2009).

4. Charles Abelmann and Richard Elmore, *When Accountability Knocks, Will Anyone Answer?* CPRE Research Report No. RR-42 (Philadelphia: University of Pennsylvania, Consortium for Policy Research in Education, 1999).

Chapter 10

1. *Medical case rounds:* Y Xiao, P Milgram, and D J Doyle, "Medical Case Rounds: A Medium for Training and Studying Real-Life Decision Making" *Proceedings of the Human Factors and Ergonomics Society Annual Meeting* 39, no. 20 (October 1995): 1330–1333; *conference room rounds:* Robert M. Wachter and Harry Hollander, *Hospital Medicine* (Lippincott Williams & Wilkins, 2005); and *multidiscipline rounds:* Charles Burger, "Multi-Disciplinary Rounds: A Method to Improve Quality and Safety of Critically Ill Patients" *Northeast Florida Medicine* 58, no. 3 (2007): 16–19.

ACKNOWLEDGMENTS

The book represents a close look at the practice of a subset of the thousands of people using rounds to help improve instruction for students. It is in appreciation of those educators, and especially the dozens of teachers and administrators who shared their experiences with me, that I offer this book. I specifically wish to thank the individuals at each of the case study sites who responded to interview questions and e-mails and more e-mails and more questions, who read drafts of the cases, supplied helpful artifacts, and related their stories with enthusiasm, candor, and generosity:

- Killingly Public Schools: Bill Silver, Marilyn Oat, Lisa Higgins, and Margaret Walker
- Pegasus School of Liberal Arts and Sciences: Virginia Lannen, Virginia Hart, and Frances Teran
- Akron Public Schools: Ellen McWilliams, Rick Sims, Sharon Hall, and Angela Harper Brooks
- Farmington Public Schools: Kathleen Greider, Bob Villanova, Alicia Bowman, Renee St. Hilaire, Kim Wynne, and Tim Breslin and the Farmington High School students and administrators courageous enough to invite me—knowing that I would write about it—on their first-ever student rounds visit
- Ballarat Clarendon College: Jan McClure, Reid Smith, Steven Belcher, and Jennifer McGie

The other big thank you goes to my rounds colleagues at Harvard. My coauthors on *Instructional Rounds in Education*, Liz City, Richard Elmore, and Sarah Fiarman, have taught me a great deal about rounds, about improvement, and about the joys of working on a wonderful team. Since the publication of the book, Stefanie Reinhorn, John Roberts, and Tim O'Brien have joined us, bringing terrific insights, energy, and perspectives. Stef and Liz were particularly helpful in sorting through some of the blurry "Is it rounds or isn't it?" issues in chapter 8. Rounds work is such a collaborative effort for me that in this book I frequently use the pronoun *we* to describe what I am thinking or doing. Notwithstanding the powerful collaborative context in which I've had the privilege to work, this is a solo-authored book, and I take full responsibility for the contents, flaws, errors, and omissions.

ABOUT THE AUTHOR

Lee Teitel teaches courses at the Harvard Graduate School of Education on leadership development; partnership and networking; and understanding organizations and how to improve them. He directs the master's-level School Leadership Program. He was the founding director and then faculty senior associate of the Executive Leadership Program for Educators, a five-year collaboration of the Harvard Graduate School of Education, Harvard Business School, and Harvard Kennedy School of Government that focused on bringing high-quality teaching and learning to scale in urban and high-need districts.

Teitel is coauthor (with Elizabeth City, Richard Elmore, and Sarah Fiarman) of *Instructional Rounds in Education: A Network Approach to Improving Teaching and Learning* (Harvard Education Press, 2009). He has facilitated or helped launch instructional rounds networks in ten states in the United States, Australia, Canada, and Sweden.

INDEX